W9-CKI-628

12.95

Father, Have I Kept My Promise?

Edith Weisskopf-Joelson

Father, Have I Kept My Promise?

Madness as Seen from Within

Edith Weisskopf-Joelson

with an Afterword by Viktor Frankl

Purdue University Press
West Lafayette, Indiana

Book designed by Eileen Rich

Produced through the cooperation of the Institute of Logotherapy

Published 1988

Library of Congress Cataloging-in-Publication Data

Weisskopf-Joelson, Edith, 1910–1983
    *Father, have I kept my promise? : madness as seen from within /
    Edith Weisskopf-Joelson ; with an afterword by Viktor Frankl.*
        p.   cm.
    Bibliography: p.
    ISBN 0-911198-93-8
    1. Weisskopf-Joelson, Edith, 1910–1983—Mental health.
    2. Psychotherapists—United States—Biography.   I. Title.
    *[DNLM: 1. Weisskopf-Joelson, Edith, 1910–1983.   2. Mental
    disorders—personal narratives.   3. Psychiatry—personal narratives.
    WZ   100   W433]*
    RC438.6.W45A3   1988
150'.92'4—dc 19
[B]
DNLM/DLC
for Library of Congress   *87-27387*
                                                                CIP

Printed in the United States of America

When I was mad I flooded the outer world with my inner life until the world disappeared and everything became dream, wish, and fantasy. But if the mad person does not become too fearful of this ocean of inner life, she will be able to withdraw the flood slowly and lovingly and see the earth again, an earth which is no longer withered and dry, an earth which is now bathed in the nectar of the human soul.

If mental illness is not an illness in the traditional sense of the word, but a condition that can be viewed as good or bad, then those who have experienced the positive aspects of madness have an important task to fulfill, namely, to change the image of the mad person in the eyes of the public. Blacks and women have made a united effort in this direction with regard to their minorities. Why could those who have experienced madness not do the same? (A start has already been made to move in this direction.)

It is hoped that this book may represent one step toward this goal, that it may give the reader a glimpse of the mysterious beauty, the terror, the sadness, and the healing rebirth brought into existence by the strange experience which we call madness.

Contents

Foreword

Within our lifetime each of us encounters a few people who leave lasting impressions even if the moments spent with them are but a fraction of life's total experiences. Edith Weisskopf-Joelson fits that description in my own history. I probably spent less than fifteen days in any kind of direct contact with her. Yet, those moments represent in my memory a rich storehouse of warmth, compassion, and a sense of freedom. I struggle to avoid telling many of the wonderful stories I associate with Edith, but I should like to share two occasions when I was privileged to be in her company.

The first of these encounters took place at the Second World Congress of Logotherapy in Hartford, Connecticut, in 1982. Dr. Viktor Frankl was unable to attend because of a recent illness, so Dr. Weisskopf-Joelson was asked to come in his stead. Her free-floating spirit and knowledge of life and logotherapy was one of the highlights of that world congress.

The second opportunity to be with her came the following year at the third world congress in Regensburg, West Germany. There she presented three papers, in English and German, and was given a standing ovation. Following the congress, my wife and I were part of a group of twenty-eight people who toured Bavaria and Austria. Edith, nattily dressed in her green Tyrolean felt hat and tailored clothes, was part of the group.

It was an awesome experience to be with her as we visited the Eagles Nest and to watch her pull open all of the doors to let the world know that Hitler was gone and that she was there to verify that no more Nazis were lingering about the premises. On that trip we also visited her hometown of Vienna. She went to see the apartment in which she grew up as a child and other places of nostalgia. She wanted to use her experiences from that trip in her future lectures and in the manuscript she was working on. Alas, it was not to be.

You could not be around Edith without realizing that she was the embodiment of logotherapy. It was difficult to distinguish where logotherapy ended and her personal lifestyle began. She was a practical person who believed that if something worked you should use it. Logotherapy worked for Edith, and she worked for logotherapy. Had she found something even better for her, I am convinced that she would have gone on to that as well.

Observing her on that trip through southern Germany and Austria was like watching a child in worldly wonderment. After a long absence from this place, she appeared to be seeking an understanding of those never-to-be-answered questions of life. After all, she was a free-floating spirit.

I never saw Edith again. On July 3, 1983, three days after her return from the trip, she died.

She left a rough-hewn autobiographical manuscript as a legacy to the Institute of Logotherapy. It was as though her parting words might have been: "I lived it, now you see what you can make of it."

Institute of Logotherapy   WILLIS C. FINCK

Acknowledgments

Our thanks go to Dr. Walter Weisskopf, Edith's brother; Michael Joelson, her former husband; and Professor James B. Klee, her literary executor, for providing missing links of information.

Our special thanks go to Sandie Ritter, the editor of this manuscript, who managed the formidable task of arranging the piles of papers left behind by Edith into a publishable whole while studying logotherapy and working at the institute.

Institute of Logotherapy   JOSEPH B. FABRY

Weisskopf-Joelson Chronology

1910	Born in Vienna, Austria, on November 29.	1950	Earns diploma in clinical psychology from the American Board of Examiners in Professional Psychology.
1937	Earns Ph.D. degree in psychology from the University of Vienna.		
1938	Emigrates from Austria.	1951	Marries Michael ("Zuzu") Joelson.
1939	Arrives in the United States.	1961	Separates from Joelson.
1939–42	Is an instructor in the Department of Psychology at Briarcliff College (New York).	1962–64	Is a tuberculosis patient at Valley View Hospital.
		1964–65	Teaches at St. Mary-of-the-Woods College (Terre Haute, Indiana).
1941	Marries Gustav Ichheiser.*	1965–66	Is a patient at Pineville Mental Hospital.
1942–49	Is an instructor and then an assistant professor in the Department of Psychology at Indiana University.	1966–67	Is a visiting professor in the Department of Psychology at Duke University.
1943	Divorces Ichheiser.	1967–78	Is a professor in the Department of Psychology at the University of Georgia. (Retires with emerita status.)
1944–48	Is a clinical psychologist in the mental health clinic of the Indiana State Department of Public Welfare.		
		1972	Divorces Joelson.
1949–65	Is an assistant professor and then a professor in the Department of Psychology at Purdue University.	1983	Dies July 3 after a series of cardiac arrests.

*Dr. Weisskopf-Joelson will mention Gustav Ichheiser's influence on her, but not that they were married.

xiii

Father, Have I Kept My Promise?

Emigration from Childhood

The door of the train compartment opens abruptly. I turn my head without lifting my eyes from the floor. I see four black boots, meticulously shining and ominously familiar. What now? I could keep my eyes down, for I suspect I already know who these people are. Instead my glance wanders upward and I see black breeches, gray tunics with shoulder stripes, one embroidered eagle atop one swastika on each left sleeve, two faces shaded by peaked, gray caps decorated with eagles perching above skulls.

These uniforms tell me that my two travelling companions are officers of the SS (*Schutzstaffel*), Nazi storm troopers who actively harrass, torture and kill Jews. The shoulder stripes indicate that the man on the right is a major and the one on the left a lieutenant. Both officers are tall, slim, and muscular, with athletic but graceful movements. They sit down on the bench facing me.

The lieutenant's face is long and narrow, with strong cheek bones, thin lips and a small nose. He wears rimless glasses covering blue and somewhat watery eyes. His skin is very light and covered with barely visible freckles. He looks meticulous and intellectual. His age is about thirty.

The major must be close to fifty years old. As he removes his cap, I see that his head is bald and shiny except for some ash-blond hair, beginning to gray, which forms a semicircle on the back of his head. His nose is long, sharp, and curved, like that of an eagle, and his eyes are so narrow that it is hard to discern their color. He too is pale, as though he had not been exposed to the sun for a long time.

My heart beats so loudly that I feel these SS officers will hear it. Then I look through the window at the platform. It is empty. Please God, let someone pass or some event happen down there so I can look away from Hitler's elite guard and not be punished for it.

And then I hear, "Heisse Würstel, heisse Würstel!" Hot dogs! It sounds more beautiful to me than the music of Mozart. The window is already open so I shout, "Hier bitte!" (Here please), and the vending woman asks, "Senf oder Kren?" (Mustard or horseradish?). When I say "Mustard," she hollers "One mark." It is only now that I realize I won't be able to pay because I only have the seven marks (three dollars) with me that the German government permits Jewish refugees to take across the border, and I'm not so foolish as to spend one-seventh of my entire fortune on hot dogs. Instead I give the vendor my whole big sheet of German stamps for the juicy food, saying, "Please take this." The lady says, "That's too much," but I sit down without answering. Of what use will German stamps be to me anyway after tonight?

When I sit down with my two hot dogs and a Kaiser roll, butterflies float in my stomach. But when I see both Nazi officers engrossed in reading *Der Völkische Beobachter,* the official Nazi newspaper, I begin to eat and to plan. The trip from Vienna to Hamburg will take fifteen hours. Should I move to another compartment? Should I read? Should I bow to the inevitable conversation with these Nazis? I take my suitcase from the rack, open it, and take out my detective novel. Then a jerk, a hiss, steam blurring the window, and soon rattata, rattata, rattata—all shake me from my novel, and the red slated roofs of Vienna, laundry hanging limply on clotheslines, and a few dark flags with swastikas remind me that my life as the only daughter of a wealthy Austrian family has come to an end. I am fleeing the Nazis, I am journeying to America. Will I make it? How will I ever manage to make it? Rattata, rattata, rattata. . . .

I return to my detective novel, *Wahnsinn (Madness),* and read until the middle-aged man, Werner, asks a beautiful widow, Hilde, to marry him. The ticket collector enters. He punches our tickets and says, "Hamburg," "Hamburg," "Hamburg." As the ticket man leaves, the major begins to talk to me.

"Do you live in Hamburg?"

I look up and decide, instantaneously, that I will view his gesture as small talk and not as an inquisition.

"No, I live in Vienna." The truth is, I should have said, "Tonight I live nowhere."

"Do you have relatives or friends in Hamburg?"

"No, I don't know anyone there."

"Perhaps you are planning to get a job?"

"No, I am not planning to do that."

Now the lieutenant to the right adds, "I bet you are a tourist on vacation. How long do you plan to stay in Hamburg?"

"Just for two hours. Then I shall catch a ship to Norway."

Both men sit up straight, chests out, bellies in. The major clears his throat and says, "You must be on official business. Otherwise, being German, you couldn't have got a permit to cross the border." (Vienna was, at that time, a German town.)

My intuition says: tell the truth.

"No, I am not on official business. I am a Jewish refugee planning to leave Germany and to settle in the United States. I hope to take a ship from Hamburg to Norway tonight. Then I shall wait in Norway until my quota number comes up—my official permission to enter the United States. In all probability this will happen in March 1939."

The two men stare at me. Then the major says, "You don't look Jewish."

"Most Jews don't look Jewish."

After a long silence the lieutenant asks, "Do you have relatives or friends in Norway?"

"No."

"Do you speak Norwegian?"

"No."

"But you do have enough money to live comfortably until March?"

I do not know whether I should laugh or cry. "I have seven marks."

The two faces show disbelief, worry and guilt.

The major: "But you don't look like a poor woman."

"I left a fortune in Vienna, but, according to German law, refugees cannot take more than seven marks out of the country."

Long silence.

I return to my book, Hilde finally marries Werner. Then I am interrupted.

The major: "But what is going to become of you? Do you think you can get a job in Norway?"

"No, I don't have the permission to work since I have only a visitor's visa."

Silence.

Soon after Hilde marries Werner she begins to suffer hallucinations: she sees her late husband, who was killed during World War I, standing in front of her bed, with a bandage around his head, looking just as he looked in the military hospital where she had visited him before his death.

I hear the two SS whispering to each other. Maybe I had better keep my eyes fixed on the book. But the two men get up abruptly from their seats and click their heels, so I look up.

"Please excuse us for being so rude. We have not even introduced ourselves. This is Lieutenant Hans Dietrich, and I am Major Horst von Schollenburg."

"My name is Edith Weisskopf."

They tell me they just cannot understand how a young woman can survive without money and without the permission to work in a foreign country from September 1938 to March 1939, and I find myself in the strange position of having to comfort two Nazi officers, to assuage their worries about me. I inform them that I am twenty-eight years old, older than I look, and that there are Jewish aid committees in many places bordering Germany, which I am sure will help me. What I do not tell them is that whatever will happen to me in Norway is infinitely better than whatever would happen to me in Germany.

In the short silence that follows, I look out the window and think about the details of my recent journey. I left Vienna in a hurry. I knew it wouldn't be difficult to cross the German border with respect to the *German* authorities. They wanted to get rid of as many Jews as fast as possible, before they decided to kill the six million who remained. But if you step out of one country, you have to step into another country, and the countries adjacent to Germany had closed their borders against the onslaught of penniless refugees.

On a Wednesday in September, I had heard that a small Norwegian ship shuttled daily from Bergen, Norway, to Hamburg, Germany, to enable the people of Bergen to shop in the large city of Hamburg. This small shipping line had never been used by refugees, since few people were aware of its existence. Thus no arrangements had been made to identify refugees and to deny them access to the ship. I packed my belongings, and the next morning I was on my way with some of my clothes, three dollars, and two ship tickets—one from Hamburg to Bergen, and one from Bergen to New York City.

It is impossible to stop them from being concerned. Soon the officers interrupt my thinking to offer me, in their concern, the most moving yet most politically naive of suggestions. For example, the lieutenant asks me if I would take a small sum of money from him. Thus I have to explain again that the problem is not that I do not *have* enough money, but that I *cannot take* enough money across the German border, neither his money nor my money.

Another moving but hair-raising suggestion: both men could accompany me to the ship to make sure that the Norwegian border won't be closed. I am planning to step on this ship very casually, trying hard not to attract attention, as if I were a Norwegian on a shopping trip. But now I see myself accompanied by two of the most conspicuously decorated, uniformed Nazis! After I explain all this to them quite carefully and tactfully, I return to my book. It turns out that Hilde's alleged hallucinations were not so crazy. What she had seen had really happened. Her late husband's double, with a bandage around his head, actually stood in front of her bed, having been hired by her second husband, who was trying to drive her insane so he could lay his hands on her money. The result: a stiff prison sentence for Werner, and discharge from the hospital and happiness for Hilde.

The whistle blows. We arrive in Hamburg.

I find myself suddenly saying, "Major von Schollenberg, Lieutenant Dietrich, you are trying to help me, and it makes me sad that I must reject your offers because you would put me and yourselves in danger. But you have already helped me without knowing that you did. You have accompanied me with love and concern to the border of your fatherland. Never before has this happened to a Jewish person. But if you want to do one more thing for me, please do whatever you can for the Jews who are left behind. *Lebt wohl!* I shall never forget you." I try to grab my two large suitcases, but the SS are faster and each of the officers grabs one.

"No, you must let me carry my own suitcases."

"But Fraulein, German officers won't let a lady carry her baggage."

What is the matter with these men? Don't they know they must not be seen in public with a Jewess? I look at them firmly, almost angrily, and say with a commanding voice, "From now on we won't be alone anymore.

People will see us and you must act as if I were a total stranger. Otherwise you could endanger your life and also mine."

"Jawohl, Fräulein."

Without looking back, I hurry to the end of the railroad car, holding my suitcases as if they were my only link to life. When I reach the stairs leading to the platform, I get some help from the conductor. Then I hurry, following the crowd, out of the railroad station into the unknown city of Hamburg. The next thing I remember is a stewardess showing me to my cabin on a small Norwegian ship.

From the moment I left the train to the moment I entered the Norwegian ship there lies an emotionally vast span of time during which I must have passed through the German customs and the Norwegian border, but these two most feared events are buried in complete forgetfulness.

I am sitting on a hard bench in a waiting room at the harbor of Bergen. It is 7:00 A.M., and cold rain is beating against the windows. The sun rises late in Norway this time of the year. It is still pitch dark and will remain dark for another two hours. My luggage is checked free of charge. I am on my own.

As I sit in this dismal place without friends, without money, without language, I begin to forget about German customs, crossing the Norwegian border, being searched for valuables, even boarding the Norwegian ship: I begin to allow blissful oblivion to swallow all of this. I feel enormous elation engulfing every cell in my body as I sit in this waiting room. I want to run, to sing, to stretch out my arms and embrace the air about me. I am free! I won't have to fear torture, persecution, and concentration camps. I am in a country where people talk to each other without terror, where they smile, where they play, where they make music.

Intoxicated with the wine of freedom, as I sit in this dismal waiting room I am seized by a sense of curiosity and adventure. I get up and run across the room, then back to my bench again. Alone in the world for the first time! Twenty-eight years old, pretty—perhaps beautiful—bright and educated, with a doctor's degree in psychology. What will the future bring? Why not stop worrying and simply jump into the whirl of a new life and see where destiny will take me? Soon, however, the euphoria wears off. Now quite soberly I have to decide just what I should do next. Step by step. First, I think I shall seek help from a Jewish emergency committee for the rescue of refugees. Is there such a committee in Bergen? How big a town is Bergen? How can I find out? Elementary, dear Edith! In the corner of the waiting room is a telephone with a directory. The directory is thin. Bergen is a small town. But it wouldn't do any harm to look under "Jewish."

I open the book trying to find the word *Jüdisch*—how silly! *Jüdisch* is the German word for Jewish, and what I need is the Norwegian word, which I don't know. In most European languages, Jewish starts with a *J*. Since it is only 7:30 and I have lots of time, I thumb through all the *J*'s. There are three pages of Johansens, but I cannot find any word that could possibly mean Jewish.

Another thought. They must have a rabbi in this town, and he could certainly be of some help. My search is in vain. But here there is an interesting name, Moshe Rabinowitz.

The time is now 9:00, it is beginning to get light, and I decide, fearlessly and recklessly, to go and see Mr. Rabinowitz. I copy the address and find my way by endless questioning: "Sprechen Sie Deutsch?" "Do you speak English?" "Parlez-vous francais?" And if the answer is "ja," "yes," or "oui," I show my slip of paper with Mr. Rabinowitz's address and ask for directions.

It is 9:30, and I stand in front of my destination—not a family home, not an apartment building, but a huge department store. Could it be that Mr. Rabinowitz is the owner of the store? I guess that the writing on the front door says that the store will open at 10:00. I wait. Then I enter and ask a salesgirl, "Moshe Rabinowitz?" When she realizes I cannot speak Norwegian, she shows me the palm of her left hand and spreads her fingers. I take this to mean that Mr. Rabinowitz's office is on the fifth floor.

It is the top floor, and I have to walk through a huge room with a blue wall-to-wall carpet and a multitude of desks with typing secretaries. At the end of the room is a glass door with the inscription MOSHE RABINOWITZ. I knock and enter. Another secretary, and behind her the door to the inner sanctum. The secretary speaks English. "May I help you?"

"I need to see Mr. Rabinowitz."

"Do you have an appointment?"

"No."

She examines her calendar. Then, with a smile, "Mr. Rabinowitz can see you next Monday at 10 A.M."

Today is Thursday. How shall I eat and sleep Friday, Saturday and Sunday?

I ask, "Is Mr. Rabinowitz in his office now?"

"Yes, but he is busy."

"Could you take a note to him right now?"

The secretary agrees reluctantly and hands me a pad of paper and a pen. I wonder in what language I should write and decide German would be my best choice. If he cannot speak German he can probably speak Yiddish, and the two languages are so similar that he'll understand me.

The secretary calls, "Hialmar, Hialmar," and a teenaged boy takes my note to the boss. Again, I feel the thrill of adventure rushing down my spine. The note says:

> *I have just arrived from Germany. I am a Jewish woman. Can you refer me to an emergency committee for help?*
>
> *Edith Weisskopf*

The phone on the secretary's desk rings almost immediately and, after exchanging a few words over the phone, the woman says, "You may go in."

Mr. Rabinowitz turns out to be a short, stocky man of about forty. He is not handsome but has an appealing smile and a good deal of warmth. He asks me to take a seat and questions me with interest and skill about my escape from Germany, about the living conditions of the German Jews, about my family, and about my plans for the future.

In turn, I find that he and his brother own several department stores and textile mills all over Scandinavia. I conclude he must be a multimillionaire. He explains there is no emergency committee in Bergen and, at the moment, he cannot give me any advice as to what I could do. "But I am going to give it a lot of thought," he adds, "and I am sure we'll find some solution."

He has to stay in the store till 5 P.M. Would I be interested in resting up in his home until then? His sister will be there and would see to it that I am comfortable.

Pretty soon I sit in the back seat of a limousine, and a uniformed chauffeur drives me to Mr. Rabinowitz's home. I feel like a figure in a Hollywood movie. Too sleepy to take in the details of the home, I become dimly aware of the general atmosphere—rich and ostentatious. The sister is hospitable, but I tell her, "No, thank you, I am too tired to eat anything." Pretty soon I fall asleep in a silk-and-ruffles bed, my last realistic thought being that Mr. Rabinowitz is a widower who lives with his sister and his twenty-year-old niece.

Five weeks later Mr. Rabinowitz asks me to marry him. My newly acquired Norwegian friends congratulate me.

"How lucky you are! A poor woman all by herself in a strange country and, whoops, she changes into a millionairess. Now you can have everything you want—a Rolls Royce, a chauffeur, mink coats, diamonds . . ."

Such little sermons cut deep into my heart, like a diamond itself, and make me feel completely alone, as if suspended in space. I seem to be able to get SS officers to worry about me, millionaires to propose to me, and yet I am absolutely unable to present myself as the kind of person I am. I couldn't care less about mink coats or diamonds. Not for one moment do I consider marrying Mr. Rabinowitz. Surely I have always wanted to get married, but mostly because society demands that women should do so, because Mother and most other people would view me as a failure were I to remain single, because I want to appear "normal" to Mother and to others.

In order to achieve this disguise of marriage, however, I must marry a suitable partner. And to Mother, that would mean only a well-educated, cultured, intellectual man. And Moshe Rabinowitz is as far from that as anyone I have previously known.

He came from a Polish ghetto to Norway about twenty years before I met him. He had come with a pushcart from which he sold sundries. Talented in enterprises, he eventually acquired department stores and textile mills in Scandinavia. He still knew very little Norwegian. He spoke

11

only Yiddish, as if he had never left the ghetto twenty years before. Furthermore, his manners were not those of a refined man. For example, when he first invited me to tea, I took one lump of sugar as I always do; but Moshe objected, saying in the manner of the newly rich, ''Take more, take three or four. We have got it. We have more food than we can eat in this house.'' Yes, he was a kind-hearted man of warmth and business sense, but I certainly could never explain him to Mother. So I told him no.

Quite some time ago, when I started to date during my late teens, I worked out a strategy which I would use in case I wanted to marry someone who did not measure up to my mother's standards. I would tell people that I was in love, irrespective of whether I was or not. Being in love was viewed as something positive. It could not eradicate lack of refinement and culture, but it could soften the heavy blow of receiving a man of lower status into the family. But, you see, even this strategy would not have worked with Moshe because nobody would be able to believe that I could fall in love with a man so different from myself. The difference in social class and education would have made love, and even the pretense of love, very difficult. So I told him no.

In February 1939 I was finally granted permission to enter the United States.

Now I stand on board a ship and wave goodbye to Moshe. Another goodbye, another tear. And behind my sadness something is pounding within me, slowly making itself known. Soon I'll be in America. Soon I'll have to be an adult. Soon I'll have to work in order to live, something which, at the age of twenty-eight, I have never done before. The something which is pounding within me is sheer, unadulterated terror.

The Promise

I was born in Vienna, Austria, in 1910. My father was first a judge and then an attorney. Mother was a homemaker.

Father died in Vienna in 1926 when I was sixteen, and Mother in New York in 1958 when I was forty-eight. She encouraged my two brothers and me to keep up appearances that went along with being cultured, intellectual, liberal, and wealthy, which we were. Indeed she prided herself on the fact that we sustained an attitude towards the world that was secular, scientific, and empirical. Although we were Jews we did not practice our religion.

To further ensure that her only daughter turned out to be a cultured, educated, and refined little lady who did everything just right, Mother focussed her formidable energy on raising me properly. She raised me to be a highbrow—not too sexy, yet popular enough with the boys to get marriage proposals.

Thus, from my earliest years, I had to wear nice clothes when going to downtown Vienna, and one day when I refused, Mother had a veritable outbreak of rage. She insisted on an upper-class appearance all through my childhood and adolescence which caused considerable trouble, especially during adolescence when, perhaps in defiance, I chose my friends among older boys with left-wing and counterculture inclinations.

Once I told Mother about one of my girlfriends' fathers, who was considered an industrial genius: he started as a pauper and built an empire within the textile industry. He was totally immersed in his work and had—in all probability—never read a book in his life. Mother said: "A person like this is hardly a human being."

Starting when I was fourteen, Mother took me on trips abroad during school vacations. The first country we visited was England.

In dining cars and restaurants, Mother would point out some woman, not with her forefinger, of course, but by a slight nod of her head, and would say: "Watch her for a while, but don't do it conspicuously. See how she gestures with her hands, while holding her fork, when she speaks. It immediately shows you that she is not a lady. And now she can't get her green peas on the fork, so what does she do? She tears off a bit of her roll and uses it to push her food up the fork. She has very bad table manners. Now look at that woman to the left. She is a real lady. Look at her clothes. Peacefully subdued colors: her whole outfit is gray, and the blouse and hat are just a little lighter than the skirt. And those beautiful simple pumps matching her purse. And very, very little makeup. Remember that." Mother attempted to make me a cultured lady.

We had read the tourist guidebook from cover to cover. Accordingly, we had spent hours at the British Museum of Art, where I learned the styles of famous British painters—of Gainsborough, Turner, and Whistler. We went to the Tower after having read the history of the terrible events which occurred there; we attended concerts and saw stage plays by Shakespeare.

Someone had planned a get-together for me and some of my classmates who were visiting London at the same time. We all met at a restaurant for dinner. I noticed that the other youngsters had not studied Gainsborough, Whistler, Turner, or Shakespeare. Instead, they had engaged in frivolous fun. Things like going to the zoo, browsing through department stores and shops, buying clothes and souvenirs, attending greyhound races, taking a trip to the beach, and watching thrillers in the cinema.

Later, when I was fifteen, Mother took me on a second trip to London, again with the aim of shaping me into a cultured and educated lady. At that time we watched the English aristocracy riding horseback in Hyde Park, and Mother commented on the straight posture and long-legged figures of British nobility. She was rather proud that her daughter, too, had long legs and straight posture, and could have been taken for a duchess.

Since approval was very important to me, I submitted to the social and cultural influence of my mother. I even became convinced that

Mother's messages were the truth and the whole truth. But now and then I wondered if there wasn't something phony, elitist, and intolerant about her standards.

My doubts arose first in the cultural-intellectual realm. Take, for example, Mother's interest in art. There was a reproduction of a painting of John the Baptist in the parlor of our home. Mother had often pointed out to me what a wonderful work of art this painting was, but had never told me what the painting represented. I suspected mother did not know who John the Baptist was, and it seemed strange that she had never tried to find out.

Of course I understood that Jews do not tend to concern themselves with the New Testament and the life of Christ. But Mother also ignored the content of art depicting scenes from the Old Testament. She explained how Michelangelo's statue of Moses with the Ten Commandments illustrates the perfection of Renaissance art, but she did not seem aware of the fact that this statue represented one of the greatest moments in history.

When we travelled together, another thing struck me about Mother's so-called cultural interests. While she was so interested in museums and historical monuments, she completely disregarded the people who inhabited the country. She was interested in people who lived several centuries ago, not in those who lived in the present. She knew nothing of the countries' political parties, about wages and employment, and about other social issues of this kind, maybe because she considered the lower classes as not truly human.

But the worst blow came one day when Mother picked up a book about population growth at Deuticke's bookstore in downtown Vienna. The book came fresh from the press, was written by a brilliant author, and contained a penetrating analysis of the dangers of overpopulation.

A week or two later, Mother and I sat in the living room. It was one of those rare moments when she let down her hair and told me about her childhood. Her family had spent many summers at the lakes which are so plentiful in the Alps. But their vacations were interrupted many times by polio epidemics which caused them to flee in panic back to the city. Whereto I said: "I wish someone would find a cure for polio."

"No, Edith," Mother replied, "you shouldn't wish that, because a cure would increase the population growth."

15

"But Mother," I whispered. This was all I could say.

Did Mother see the death and crippling of children as a solution for overpopulation? Was Mother a woman without heart? No, she had a heart all right, but she could not apply what she read to what her heart told her, and, thus, did not truly understand what she was reading.

There was more: Mother was unable to talk to me about anything pertaining to love and sex. Once, when I was twelve, I was returning from a walk with my father. I felt tired, as if I were coming down with a cold. I undressed and put on pajamas.

When I had taken off my panties, I noticed that they were soiled with large brownish-red spots. I thought I had passed a bowel movement without noticing it, and like a small child, I took my panties to my mother and held them up for her to see. She looked at me sadly and said: "Oh, already? You are only twelve."

She had never told me about menstruation, and even now she did not explain. All she said was, "This is blood, and you are going to bleed for a few days. It is not a disease. All grown-up women bleed like this once a month. It is called 'being unwell.' Let's go to my bedroom and I'll show you how to keep the blood from spotting your clothes."

That was all. No explanation of where the blood came from. No hint that what I experienced was connected with the process of reproduction.

Eight years later I fell in love, and for the first time experienced the intimacy of sex. I kept my relationship a secret from Mother for several months. But finally she began to ask questions, and I told her the whole truth, to which she replied: "But don't you know that one doesn't do such things?" It was said with the same facial and vocal expression with which she might say: "Don't you know that a lady wears gloves when she goes downtown?"

My mother was independently wealthy and had fixed views on the social etiquette of a lady in Viennese society, and upon her role within the family. It always started like this: we would be sitting at the dinner table. The bell would ring, the maid would open the door and, after a very brief interchange of words, appear in the dining room and announce that a stranger wished to speak to the head of the household.

Mother would ask, "Is it a male or a female?"

"A male, ma'm."

"A man or a gentleman?"

16

If the answer was "A gentleman," my mother would be justified to assume that the maid had asked him to take a seat in the spacious foyer. Then mother would go immediately to ascertain the gentleman's identity and the purpose of his visit. Depending on the circumstances, she might ask him to join us for dessert and coffee.

If, however, the maid's answer was "A man," my mother could be sure that the maid had left him standing outside the door. In that case my mother would order the maid to get the man's name and ask him what he wanted without ever permitting him to enter. In most cases the man turned out to be a poor Jew who had been sent by the Jewish welfare agency to ask for money. The maid would be asked to bring Mother's purse and, with a facial expression which people assume when they smell a bad odor, Mother would take a sizeable bill out of the wallet and hand it to the man—carefully, touching it with two fingers only, as if the bill itself would be covered with the repugnant dirt associated with poverty.

A similar course of events would take place if the visitor turned out to be a female. Then the question would be: "Is it a woman or a lady?"

Apparently there were no borderline cases, since the maid never hesitated when answering these questions.

Thus I learned that there were gentlemen and ladies who are fully human and are to be treated as such. And then there are the common people, men and women, who are to be supported by charity if necessary, but are to be viewed as lower forms of Homo sapiens. Among these lower forms there was a further hierarchy. Poor Jews were a wee bit lower than poor Christians, and among poor Jews there was a caste of "untouchables": the orthodox Jews with long beards, sideburns and caftans who had been driven out of Poland or Russia by cruel persecution and who sought refuge in the Jewish district of Vienna called Leopoldstadt. They often could not speak any language other than Yiddish or Hebrew. Some of these tried to live on meager profits from selling "sundries," which they pushed through the streets on carts. Mother warned me never to touch these wares because they were full of germs.

Father, by contrast, did not share Mother's snobbishness; in fact he tried to teach me values in direct opposition to her artificial ones. He tried to teach me to love and respect all people and to honor God. Father never joined us on our trips because he was too busy. Although he worked long hours as an attorney to support Mother in the style which she enjoyed, he managed to spend time with his daughter, whom he loved with a bashful intensity. We used to take walks in the Vienna Woods and engage in long and serious conversations which my father skillfully adapted to my changing age.

He often said: "The most important thing is to be a good person." And seeing my questioning look, he would elaborate: "You must not only think of yourself. You must love your mother, and your teachers, and your friends. And, above all, you must love God."

One time he had told me about the meeting between Moses and God on Mount Sinai and how God gave Moses ten commandments which every human being must obey. "What are the commandments, Daddy?" I asked, and Daddy stated one or two commandments which were easy to understand when I was little, and more complex ones as I grew up, until he had covered all ten.

When I reached the age of fifteen, he reiterated the sixth commandment, "Thou shalt not kill," and asked me whether I thought it was all right to kill the enemy during combat. I said, "Yes," and Father looked at me very sadly.

I wanted to be moved by his words, but I could not do it because I felt the image of my mother looking over my shoulder, and like Mother, I thought Daddy was old-fashioned. Why couldn't he be smooth and elegant like she was? I would even imagine hearing her say during our long walks (a familiar saying of hers), "Herb, don't you know that one doesn't talk to children like this?"

When they went to a restaurant or to a resort hotel, Mother would always correct Daddy and say things like: "Herb, don't put the tip on the tablecloth, put it on the silver tray and add another schilling."

It almost seemed that Moses and the Ten Commandments had lost their power over me because the man who taught me the words of God did not have good table manners!

But later the seed that Father put into my mind began to disturb my peace. A rumble of this disturbance became faintly audible to me in the first part of the 1940s, when World War II was raging: when I taught middle-class students rather than debutantes from upper-class families; when blacks became my students as well as my colleagues; when Gustav Ichheiser, a friend of mine, made value-laden statements which demanded agreement or disagreement. The rumble became louder and louder until it turned into the song, the march, the hymn of my existence. I found that I could not stand in front of students whose eyes are asking whither with such urgency, and teach them what *is* without suggesting what *ought to be*. My thoughts began to wander more and more towards moral and spiritual values and towards the man who had instilled me with these values long before I was mature enough to understand. And, as I emulated Father's fierce sense of fairness and justice, I finally could love him. But it was too late. How happy we could have been if we had shared this love when he was still alive. Then, one day, my feelings became so strong that I felt compelled to write a letter to him, a letter which I finished fifty-three years after his death.

Dear Father,

My first remembrance of you goes back to when I was four years old and you visited me in the hospital in Vienna. My head was wrapped in white bandages covering both ears, which hurt badly from a double mastoid operation. You had been drafted into the Austrian Army to help fight World War I. My mother called you long-distance to tell you that I had to be operated on and that I might be deaf for the rest of my life. And then you came back to see me!

I remember so well. I remember how you looked in your uniform, which was all blue—not light blue and not dark blue, but something in-between. Your jacket had a stiff, navy-blue collar that went up to your chin; and there was a soldier's cap on your head—and now the most important thing: you wore a belt with a long, shining sabre attached to it. And somewhere there was something red on your uniform, but I can't remember what it was. I believe you were a lieutenant. Oh, and then there was the moustache—so beautifully groomed—and when you kissed me it tickled.

I felt as if Saint Whoever had descended on a cloud to visit. I was so proud, Vati (a diminutive of *Vater*, meaning Father)—that you would leave World War I, where you were supposed to smash the French, the British and the Russians, just to come and worry about whether I could hear or not. Well, it turned out I could—the surgery had not damaged my hearing.

Then you disappeared and all there was left was Mother and my two brothers. It was hard being in the hospital and knowing you were so far away. When you were home I always felt protected, but now I was scared to death that my big brothers would take my toys away and that Mother wouldn't help me because she always sided with the boys.

I have no memories covering the next four years of your life. You must have written letters to Mother, which she must have read to us, but I cannot recall any such letters.

We children were very patriotic, and that might have been in part because we thought that the side on which our Vati fought must be the right side. We sang some wild songs against Charlie (*Charlie* was a slang word we used for the Americans; it means the enemy against whom we fight a war. But now I am getting all mixed up because you and I and all of us, the Austrians and the Germans, *we* were Charlie in World War I.

But most of our wild songs were not directed against the Americans, because we knew little about them and because the songs had been made up before the States entered the war in 1917. Here is an example of our songs:

> *Jeder Schuss einen Russ,*
> *Jeder Stoss einen Franzos,*
> *Und die Flotte ist nicht faul,*
> *Schlägt den Britten um das Maul.*
> *(Every shot a Russian,*
> *Every hit a Frenchman,*
> *And the Navy never rests,*
> *Hits the mugs of the British pests.)*

We also played war games with tin soldiers and, of course, our side always won.

I guess it was the governess who made us do these nasty things (at least they seem nasty now). She created patriotism in us by what psychologists call conditioning. It worked this way: there was a fortress named Przemysl, located in what is now Poland. The fortress belonged to us. Then it was conquered by the Russians; that day the governess did not give us any dessert for dinner. Soon we reconquered the fortress and received one of our favorite desserts: strawberries with whipped cream.

Other fortresses were conquered or lost, and accordingly, we received an outstanding dessert or no dessert at all. It did not take too long until we became bloodthirsty patriots.

Toward the middle of the year 1917, Mother received a telegram from the war department saying that you had been captured by the Russians and had become a prisoner of war. From then on we spoke about you, Vati, from

20

morning to night, and usually in great fear that the Russians would mistreat you.

Then, in 1918, only a few weeks before the armistice, an event of such enormous power occurred that it has reverberated in my memory ever since. On that day the doorbell rang. It might have been morning, afternoon, or evening. It was the maid's day off, and I was asked to see who was there. I opened the door without removing the chain, as I had been taught to do. I looked and saw one of "them," one of those Jews with long caftans, beards and sideburns: "ein Polnischer."

There was a strap around his shoulders that held a large wooden tray filled with pens, pencils, small notebooks, thread, needles, toothpaste, toilet water, candy and other merchandise. I stammered: "Just a moment," slammed the door, and ran to find my mother. "Mutti (diminutive of *Mutter,* meaning Mother), Mutti, a man is outside, not a gentleman at all, a dirty Polish one."

"Did you close the door?"

"Yes, of course."

"Quick, get my purse."

And with that facial expression of superiority, which I had seen so often, she took a bill out of her wallet, handed it to me, and said, "Be sure not to remove the chain. And don't touch his hands when you give him the bill."

I ran back to the door, opened it a tiny bit, threw the bill on his tray and was about to slam the door when I felt resistance. The Polish Jew held the door open with his right hand. Is he going to tear the chain? Is he going to enter by force, to burglarize, to kill . . . ?

He did not move. He looked at me with a big smile.

"Bist *Du* die Edith?" (Are *you* Edith?)

"Yes," I whispered.

And then you said, "I am your father!"

I had to get used to you very slowly, so slowly that the process of acceptance was only half completed in 1926, the year of your death—eight years after I had contemptuously thrown money on your tray as if you were a beggar.

Acceptance became somewhat easier when you told us, in daily installments around the dinner table, the story of your escape. You were determined to escape because it was the duty of every prisoner. Your determination to do your duty was in no way influenced by your belief that the end of the war was very close. You risked your life by creeping underneath a

21

row of half-a-dozen trains, any one of which could have started its journey and crushed you to death.

And, most important as far as I was concerned, you were not really one of those contemptible Polish orthodox Jews who were so far beneath my poised and elegant mother. No, you were not. You had to assume the disguise of a Jewish peddler so no one would recognize you as an escaped prisoner. And it never occurred to you, Father, to change your disguise before you came home. For how could you have known that your family had turned against their own people, against their roots?

During the years following 1918, you caused me much embarrassment. The day after your return, you went to the barber and had him shave off your beard and your sideburns. After that you tried several kinds of moustaches, all of which looked a bit ridiculous, especially the waxy one that turned up on both ends. Why could you never look like other people?

And why could you never behave like other people? You wanted to know and see everything your little daughter did. November 29, 1919, was my ninth birthday. You insisted upon coming to the school of calisthenics, where all the kids from good families went, to watch me do exercises. I was using golden bars, like all the kids did on their birthdays.

You came with Mother and sat in the balcony watching me. She was so poised and never attracted my attention or anybody else's. But you, by golly! You turned around and said to the people behind you: "Watch her, the one with the golden bar; she's my little daughter." Then you waved to me. How could you embarrass me so much?

Why couldn't you be smooth and elegant like Mother? Why couldn't you have been born in glorious Vienna like mother and us children, instead of that Bohemian village that no one ever heard of?

And why did you give me never-ending sermons about being good, dutiful and loving? Why did you have to teach me the Ten Commandments and ask me—one by one—if I obeyed them? Didn't you know that only unenlightened people believed in God's existence?

Later you did a few things I liked. You started to make our dinner conversations really interesting. You were then a judge in some court; and you made up trials, between two feuding parties, for us children. Then you asked us to be the judges, to state our verdict and to explain how we arrived at this verdict. At the end of the "trial" you often said to Mother: "The little one always hits the nail on the head." I enjoyed the game and was flattered by your praise.

Then in 1926 you came down with pleurisy. You were lying in bed with a high fever, and the perspiration was running down your face. I was standing by your bed with many towels wiping the perspiration off your forehead. I was then sixteen years old. You pleaded over and over: "I want no one else to do that for me. Only my little daughter." Even though Mother was not present, I still felt as if she were looking over my shoulder and saying to you, "Don't you know that you shouldn't speak like this to a sixteen-year-old girl?"

Then you went to the hospital for surgery—they didn't have any antibiotics at that time. And after the surgery you died. The doctors said it was a heart attack. Your heart had been weakened through the strain of combat, imprisonment and escape. You, a full-blooded Jew, died for Germany!

But before you died I sat at your bedside in the hospital, and you said, "You must promise me . . ." And I promised.

For most of my life I forgot what I had promised.

Forgive me, Father.

Forgive me for having looked down upon the Jews with caftans, beards and sideburns. Those Jews with their sad eyes who are a part of me, a part which I could not accept.

Forgive me for having looked down on you because you came from poor and lowly parents.

Forgive me for having eyes that could not see how much you loved me.

Forgive me for having ears that could not hear the voice that taught me truth and faith and justice.

Forgive me that I could not love you.

After you died there was no pain, just emptiness, an emptiness that lasted many years. And then, from the tiny seed that you had planted in my growing mind, sprang a green twig, first small, then bigger, and finally the twig grew into a tree. The tree is strong and firm and straight; it is the tree of life, the tree of kindly, compassionate values, the tree of my own new life.

Look at the tree, Father, and answer the one burning question in my heart:

Father, have I kept my promise?

23

My Call
to Academia

I never slept—at least, that is what I thought when I was three to five years of age. The transition between being awake and then falling asleep in the evening, and between being asleep and then waking up in the morning must have been so smooth that I did not become aware of it. Nor was I aware of the long, black time called night. I thought that I went to bed every evening and got up after a while without any change in my state of consciousness. I asked my mother several times, "What does sleep mean?" or "How does it feel to sleep?" but she either dismissed my questions as a joke or gave me an answer such as, "Sleeping is what you do at night." Neither of these answers helped me solve my problem. But my supposed lack of sleep did not worry me. Rather, I kept it as a sweet secret, and perhaps I was proud of being different.

During those years I also harbored the notion that I was a child and would remain a child as long as I lived, just as my parents, two tall adults, would remain adults for as long as they lived. In other words I saw childhood as a permanent state in those possessing it. I guess I liked my role as a child and found it hard to imagine myself playing the role of an adult, shouldering responsibilities and taking care of others. Again, I accepted this notion, so alien to the way others understood the nature of human life, as a mark of my differentness from others, and I was somewhat proud of it. During my early school years, I observed other notions, feelings and experiences I had that convinced me little by little that I was different from others. For example, although I was considered by others a very bright, even brilliant student, I found myself wondering if I were not mentally retarded.

I suffered this painful doubt because, while I found it very easy to remember the readings our teacher specifically assigned us, nevertheless I found it very hard to keep up with other children in and out of school. The conversation drifted towards facts that I had not been explicitly assigned to remember.

As I moved into adolescence, this problem intensified, and I found it even harder to sustain an interest in, and thus to learn about, the outside world—the world of main streets and side streets, the world of newspapers, and books not assigned in school. The world of boys flirting with girls, and girls buying cosmetics and standing in front of the mirror applying lipstick as if they were applying their future. The subject wasn't covered in class, so I didn't know about it. Rather, I turned inward taking residence in my own private world of flamboyant fantasies of love and achievement.

Later, one of my university professors probably sensed my problem and tried to help me overcome it by suggesting I read a very simple book about how inferiority feelings motivate one to excel and to develop an interest in and loyalty to one's community. When this professor, now also my friend, suggested I discuss the book with her, all I could say was: "How does one go about making up a subject index to a book?" It seems I had absolutely no curiosity about the gist of it.

I did enjoy fiction as long as it was quite easy to read, and as long as it dealt with the problems I saw in my own life. And I enjoyed movies. But I simply did not nurture within myself any real interest in the flesh and texture, the substance of real life around me.

After the age of about fifteen, however, my intellectual difficulties ceased to bother me, because I was no longer required to be intelligent. Instead, growing into young womanhood, I was expected to be beautiful. And so my ambitions changed: I no longer wanted others to call me by my high school nickname, Socrates; rather, I wanted to be thought of as a great beauty. I became obsessed with being beautiful, in fact.

I was one of the first women in the world to have my nose "fixed" by the very surgeon, Dr. Jacques Joseph of Berlin, who developed this plastic-surgery procedure. The surgery took place in 1932. While my only reason for undergoing this operation was my desire to look pretty, it is ironic that I might not be alive today had I not had my nose changed from its original shape and its stereotypic Jewish curve. My surgery took place just six years before Hitler marched through Austria, ordering that

25

people who "looked Jewish" be picked up on the streets and taken to concentration camps, years before he carried out his systematic extermination of the Jews.

My new nose, the rosiness of my cheeks, and the smoothness of my skin, however, did not make me feel any more connected to the world than before. In fact I felt increasingly alien to it. So I began to steep myself in the abstract world of mathematics and logic. Here, my status as a "stranger to real life" was no longer a handicap.

As time went on, I came to feel more and more like I was from another planet and knew nothing about life on earth. I could therefore excel in subjects that demanded no such knowledge. This feeling penetrated my college years, so I began to major in a mathematical-type branch of philosophy called "logical positivism," which is entirely abstract and does not deal with the real world. And like that visitor from another planet, my mind was not preoccupied by facts and impressions of "real life on earth," so I did excel in this field. But despite great praise from my famous teachers, I found myself drawn more and more into my inner world, my world of personal feelings and fantasies. While intellectualized explanations, such as the one my professor-friend had suggested to me earlier, had never captured my imagination, now I found that a new school of psychology did speak directly to my subjective reality, the private world wherein I was so much at home. I received my Ph.D. in psychology in 1937.

And now I want to skip several years and many miles, and a period of awesome terror which, this time, was not private terror, but shared terror. The terror which I am skipping is the invasion of Austria by Hitler's army in 1938. No one very close to me was killed, and so the horrors of this period were not as traumatic for me as for others.

Skipping all this, I will take you directly to New York City, where I arrived as a refugee in 1939, at the tail end of the depression. It was difficult to find work, especially for recently arrived refugees. Many prominent intellectuals were servicing elevators or loading trucks. By sheer luck, I found a position within a few weeks after my arrival in March, even though I was not scheduled to start work until September. This position was that of an instructor in psychology at Briarcliff College, close to New York City. I signed the contract but was very much afraid to take the position in this new country, teaching in a new language.

For the preparation of my lectures an acquaintance recommended six books I could use as texts. Since I had never taught before and did not speak English too well, and since I was a very slow reader, I found myself suddenly alone during an incredibly hot and humid summer in New York City with six companions which, irrationally, I feared almost as much as I feared Hitler: six very abstract psychology books in English. When I opened my eyes in the mornings and saw the six books on the table, I often felt like closing my eyes again and going back to sleep.

The following months were dismal and meaningless. For at least eight hours a day I stared at page after page, preparing for my lectures. American psychology was so different from the psychology I had learned in Vienna, that I failed to find any connection between the material I was supposed to teach and my inner world—my thoughts, fantasies and wishes. The books described complex theoretical schemes which seemed to have been constructed for the purpose of making psychology look like an exact science rather than a tool for increasing our understanding of human beings' thoughts, feelings, attitudes and behaviors. This alienation from the new subject matter, combined with my strange reading disability, resulted in my not understanding much of what I read. In despair I cried, "What shall I do? How can I teach these classes?"

The months of preparation in the sweltering heat of New York City were, for me, an experience of extreme estrangement and isolation: new country, new language, no friends, and incomprehensible books. So I escaped. I spent many dismal days looking forward to the corner store's chocolate milkshakes, to escapant movies, to getting drunk on crème de cacao in my tiny room. I gave relatively little thought to the total shape of my life: to my future, or to ways in which I could improve my psychological condition.

September came, and I taught my classes. I found various ways in which I could ease my load. First, I found new books that were closer to life (and made easier reading) to enliven my lectures. Second, I emphasized the sections of psychology which were factual, rather than theoretical or philosophical. The former were easier to understand and easier to transform into lectures. For example, I expanded the biological aspects of heredity and spoke at length about chromosomes and genes.

I expanded the section on hormones and spoke at length about Pavlov's dog and how he was conditioned to salivate at the sound of a bell. I advanced very slowly to make it easy for myself, since I had an incredibly heavy teaching load.

My fears proved to be well grounded. When I gave my first test, I discovered that my students had learned very little from me. One student stormed into my office in a rage and screamed at me, "We don't understand you, and you don't understand us." She was absolutely right, and I felt deeply hurt.

Now I must implore you, Dream Reader, not to skip the next page or two. For up to now, in order to be truthful, I had to present myself as a self-centered alien, a stranger to earth life, a failure. But now let me take you by the hand and show you how I changed my ways. I stopped consoling myself with milkshakes and movies and the alcohol in crème de cacao. I stopped steeping myself in my own mind. I stopped risking feelings of alienation with deeper and more convoluted fantasies. Rather, I spent the following summer attending a series of workshops on various areas of psychology offered at Vassar College. Everything seemed real, concrete, and most interesting. I learned how to teach in America, I browsed through textbooks and other materials, and in the evenings I walked through the beautiful campus of Vassar with a young woman who taught psychology at Brooklyn College. We became friends and still are friends, and she, too, helped me in my profession.

I went through all this trouble trying to become a good teacher for a reason that I have not told you yet: I did not become a teacher only because I had to eat. Instead, it had been my ardent wish since I was seven years old to teach, to teach, to teach. And in almost every class in which I had sat as a pupil listening to the teacher I had thought: "I could present this better."

It was my special ambition to bring the material taught close to the experience of my students. I wanted to help them overcome the split between knowledge and feeling which had plagued me all my life, and at the same time I wanted to overcome my own split. And I believe that I succeeded later on.

It was my teaching which taught me to read. I can now read nonfiction, but only if I know that I am reading for my students—to present what I have read to them. And later, when I worked in graduate schools of large universities, where I had to "publish or perish," I learned that I can also read in order to prepare myself to write.

It seems miraculous that I could turn my intellectual disabilities into assets. I never could easily understand things which are expressed in too scholarly a manner, too "high falutin'," and too abstract. I must translate what I read into plain English and add a few examples. Only then can I understand without undue effort. And this necessity, for my own understanding, to translate difficult language or jargon into plain English and to clarify abstractions by concrete examples, was exactly what my students needed.

My second year at Briarcliff College, 1940–41, went well, and the yearbook was dedicated to me, which showed that I was accepted by the students. From then on, my awareness and understanding of psychological and social problems increased; as a result I could give more and more to my students. And soon it happened that students, wherever I taught, were not asking to enroll in a specific course; instead they asked, "What is Weisskopf teaching this semester?"

I had won a real victory, not a Pyrrhic one, like it would have been had I married a doctor because Mother wanted me to. It was my own bud which had bloomed into a flower, and this is the greatest gift that God can give.

And now it occurs to me that I have not told you in sufficient detail why I wanted to be a teacher. My daydream of becoming a teacher started at the age of seven and became even stronger in high school. As I briefly mentioned before, it always seemed to me that my teachers were unable to connect the subject matter taught with the personal lives of the students. I still remember one example at the age of eleven: in foreign history we studied the American Civil War and learned that Abraham Lincoln freed the "Negroes" from slavery. The teacher lectured, and we took detailed notes. The next class in foreign history started, as usual, with a brief summary of the previous lecture to be given by a randomly selected student. It happened that I was selected for this role on that day. I had studied my notes and thus could regurgitate the lecture faultlessly. My grade for this per-formance was Very Good, or One, which was the best possible grade in Austrian schools. And yet I did not understand in the least what I was saying. The Negroes in America were liberated? There were no Negroes in Austria, and I did not know that there were Negroes in

America. If so, how could they live in a country that seemed even more civilized than Austria? Did they run around among the skyscrapers wearing nothing but loincloths? I had never seen a black person in real life, but I had seen many anthropological films at the Community University in Vienna. Thus, for me, Negroes were people who lived in Africa in small primitive tribes of fishermen or hunters.

Oh, but how meaningful could all this knowledge have become if the teacher would have connected our lives with the material she taught. For example, she might have said that at present (about 1921) the social position of the black minority in the United States had much in common with the social position of the Jewish minority in Austria. And since our class consisted of about one-third Jews, one-third anti-Semitic gentiles, and one-third neutral or friendly gentiles, the American scene might have become a mighty interesting subject for little Austrian girls.

Moreover, most of the families of my classmates had one or several maids. At that time service was cheap in Europe, and even families of moderate means could afford servants. These servants tended to be women from peasant families who had migrated to the city without having learned any skills other than agricultural and domestic work. There were no laws regulating the relationship between domestic servant and employer. Servants were at the disposal of the employers twenty-four hours a day. An electric bell was located in every room of our apartment, and I could push the button day and night if I happened to need our Klara. And if our teacher had been a bit wiser, she could have helped me understand that I was treating another woman as if she were a slave. As it were, I was a slave owner. And all that understanding could have come about by truly understanding the Civil War in the United States. (Incidentally, while I was glad to have been graded Very Good on the American Civil War, I felt there was something wrong if a student, who admittedly did not understand what she was talking about, could make a good grade by mere regurgitation.)

Thus, I learned to swim by being thrown into the water. I learned to read and to make sense out of what I read by the sheer necessity of giving one or more fifty-minute lectures—sometimes every day, sometimes several times a week—to a class of students, many of whom knew more about the world than I did since they were not afflicted (or blessed?) by my lack of worldliness and of attention to what was going on. I still had difficulties trying to grasp an entire book as a whole and to understand how parts of the book were interrelated to each other as well as to the whole book. Therefore, my lectures tended to focus on several especially interesting ideas within a book, or within a comprehensive topic, rather than on the whole topic. This subterfuge may have resulted in some loss of insight for my students.

Around this time I met a very unusual man named Gustav Ichheiser. He had been born in Poland and had received his higher education at the University of Vienna, but I met him in Chicago through Else, our common friend. His fields were the social sciences with special emphasis on social psychology and sociology. He has written numerous articles published in scientific journals and one book that I know of, entitled *Appearances and Realities*. He used to expound on his theories with immense brilliance and intensity and a good deal of arrogance, saying that people were blind regarding their understanding of themselves and of others and that he wanted to open their eyes. His book must have been his last attempt to do so.

Now why am I telling you about this man? Because he had more influence on my intellectual development than any other person (except possibly Viktor Frankl, author of *Man's Search for Meaning)*. He advanced me many miles on my way from intellectual malfunction to intellectual functioning, from a pretense-psychologist, an as-if teacher and a pseudowriter to a real psychologist, a real teacher, and a real writer.

Many of my teachers in Vienna were very famous people—such as Moritz Schlick, Charlotte Bühler, Egon Brunswick, Else Frenkel-Brunswik—and I have often been asked about their influence on my present thinking. Perhaps because of my indifference towards ideas at that time, I have had to say that most of the thoughts of these people have not impressed me greatly. But not so with Gustav Ichheiser.

His conversations with me were almost exclusively directed towards opening my eyes. Until I met him, I had viewed what social scientists wrote as true and myself as good if I understood it and believed it. But Gustav stressed that social scientists are a group of people with common backgrounds, and therefore with common views. And many of the so-called truths which I taught my students were common prejudices of social scientists who live mostly in towns rather than in the country, who are mostly white rather than black, who are mostly men rather than women and, above all, who have been treated well by the existing social order.

31

Now I want to tell you in what way Gustav Ichheiser awakened me. First, he changed me from a passive reader to an active reader. I became a searcher. Every page became a question. Who are you, Author? What makes you say this? I became a detective. And if you care to finish my book, you shall see how much I like detective work. Gustav Ichheiser's view of the entire world was drenched in doubt. He said, "Things are not as they seem to be," and this sentence aroused my passion.

But at that time there was one myth which I was not able to debunk. There was one field in which I thought that things were what they seemed to be: the field of mental illness. I was convinced that normality was what it was said to be and that it was good. And that abnormality was a disgrace and shameful. And that I would be normal even if it killed me!

Second, Gustav Ichheiser aroused a passionate antagonism within me. What he said was often smug and arrogant. And thus another purpose was added to my work: to prove that many of his opinions were wrong.

In 1942 I became assistant professor of psychology at Indiana University and, two years later, also clinical psychologist at the Indiana State Department of Public Welfare. As time went on, teaching became more and more a personal activity for me. No longer did I wear the mask of a professor in order to impress people, including myself; instead, I drenched my courses with personal meaning, my own opinions and insights. Yet, the process had not gone far enough because I was still afraid every Monday that, before the week was over, my professional mask would crack and the "mentally retarded" nonreader of my early years would become apparent. Thus, my life vacillated between fear and relief. The relief on Friday of having made it for another week was one pleasure in my life which kept me going.

In 1949 a new activity entered my life, namely, research and publishing. I had accepted the position of associate professor of psychology in the graduate school at Purdue University. My first published research dealt with a test consisting of a series of pictures which psychologists used to evaluate personality. The person to be evaluated was asked to tell a story about each picture, a story which was said to reveal the storyteller's preoccupations, worries, joys and hopes. In my research I systematically changed various features in the picture to see what difference that would produce in the stories told. In this manner I wanted to find out what kind of pictures would elicit the most revealing stories and thus reflect the storyteller's personality most completely and most accurately. Pictures of this kind would be most useful to clinical psychologists who wanted to know what kind of persons their patients were and in what ways they might help them.

My research was carried out with great accuracy and with an abundance of quantitative analyses, which means with an abundance of numbers and computations. So you see, I went back to the time of my high school days when I liked to deal with numbers in order to avoid dealing with the real world.

I published many articles of this kind in a very short time. They were highly praised by my readers, and within about two years I had made a name for myself. I was made full professor of psychology. Strangely enough I was rather depressed during this time of success. I felt that the pretended accuracy of my research and, even more, the abundance of numbers and computations, were concessions to the trend of psychology at that time. I had conformed in order to become well known and respected.

At that time I came across the early writings of Viktor Frankl, who had been released in 1945 from German concentration camps and published his ideas on existential psychotherapy in many books and articles during the late forties. Many of these books still have not been translated into English. His writings supported my hunch that psychotherapy works because the therapist helps the patient develop a philosophy of life that dares to go beyond the body and the psyche. Frankl's therapy (which he called "logotherapy," or therapy through meaning) made use of the resources of the human spirit, which prominently included a will to find meaning, to have goals, and to make commitments. He saw the nature of his patients not only determined by their past, including traumas, but also determined by their future—goals and tasks that pulled them forward. It was a therapy closer to philosophy than to science. I also compared some of his psychotherapeutic cures with religious conversion, although Frankl never used religious terms. Now if there was anything from which the mainstream psychologists shied away, it was philosophy and religion. These two fields had given birth to pre-Freudian psychology; they were its parents. Now psychology had become an adolescent, later a young adult, tending to rebel against its parents. Thus I decided to do a new kind of research and a new kind of writing, based on intuition

33

more than on numbers and computations. This new philosophical approach also entered my teaching and influenced my students.

A number of psychologists in the western states gave me some recognition, but at that time, those I worked with at Purdue were strict experimentalists who vehemently rejected my new approach. Thus, my position among my colleagues dropped within a short time from stardom to complete rejection and isolation. At that time it seemed to me that if you wanted to live in a society, you had to disregard your inner promptings and follow the common trend. In order to live, you had to become an as-if person, a pretense person, a pseudoperson.

The dirty looks and snide remarks which I received when shedding my pseudoscientific skin, to emerge as a philosopher, gave me pain and flattened my inspiration. And then I found a wonder drug which pumped it up again like a balloon. A woman friend asked me if I had ever taken Benzedrine. I hadn't. She found it hard to get going in the mornings unless she took a capsule. I also found the mornings hard. But could I risk taking a drug that was unknown to me?

"Why don't you try it? Here is a capsule. Take it right after you awake; if you take it later, you might find it hard to fall asleep at night."

"What shall I do in case I like it?"

"Then get yourself prescriptions. Most any doctor will agree if you just say you are tired or depressed. No, you don't have to return my pill; forget about it and enjoy."

I went to bed with anticipation of a forthcoming adventure. When the alarm clock rang, I rose and swallowed the pill with a glass of water. Then I sat down and wrote a story. Thoughts fell upon me like red leaves in autumn. My pen could not keep up with these most precious gifts. I was a vessel receiving ideas and putting them on paper. Slow down, oh donor, please slow down: don't let me miss a single one of your enchanting favors.

Three hours later I sat in the library for the purpose of preparing my lectures for the coming week. But on the table next to me there was a book on the history of the civil war in Spain. "Today is only Tuesday," I thought, "and I have lots of time to prepare my lectures for next week." I opened the book on Spain and read, with normal speed and great involvement, for two or more hours. The reading disability which had plagued me all my life was gone!

And Benzedrine or any other amphetamine (a group of medications which elicit temporary alertness, wakefulness and elation) made me feel like the person I was meant to be. For the first time in my life, I was quivering with interest in almost everything that came my way. And I was extroverted and talkative, oh so talkative!

At that time, during the forties and fifties, the use of amphetamines on campuses was popular—comparable with the use of marijuana and alcohol today. At social gatherings, pills were passed around like cookies.

Oh yes, now I remember the strangest thing about these pills: one capsule of amphetamines made a religious person out of me. I felt the truth contained in all religions. I understood the Holy Bible, Upanishads, Koran, and Talmud.

Oh Sacred Pill, how wondrous you are: you gave me new ideas, gave me feelings, you gave me God and even gave me love for others. But you also put me in a conflict I could not resolve. So many of my colleagues held that thoughts and feelings and desires are nothing but chemical processes in our brains. Changing the chemistry can change the person. Show me the pill you take and I shall tell you who you are. And ever since I took the first fateful Benzedrine, it seemed that they were right. But this is not the way I want to look at humankind. If we are nothing but a multitude of test tubes, I don't want to live! Thus, I was torn asunder. The taking of my pills made me the person I wanted to be, but also forced me to believe in a view of life which I despised. What should I do?

Life gave me the answer. Soon I needed more and more sacred pills to be the person I was meant to be. And then I reached the stage when I could work at school and home only with the greatest effort. "Drugs," says Alan Watts, "are like a telephone receiver. You get the message, and then you put it down." What is the message? That there exist altered states of consciousness which every one of us is able to achieve, states which carry us beyond the usual way in which we see the world, which make us see the new, the wondrous, the divine. And we can do it without drugs. But this discovery came to me when I was no longer mad.

And exactly at the time when my mode of thinking, writing, and teaching was rejected by my closest colleagues, my mode of loving was rejected by my husband. The real person in me was no longer accepted by those close to me. Again it seemed to me that if I wanted to reenter my marriage and my profession, I had to play the role prescribed by

35

society. And that was when my body opened itself to the tuberculosis bacilli which had been lurking—as it were—like vultures over a battlefield. I opened myself to the bacilli to be carried into the land of silence, where I remained from 1962 to 1964. But more about that later. Now I must tell you about my husband.

Zuzu

The date was December 27, 1951, more than twelve years after I had arrived in the United States. The place was a city located within commuting distance of Purdue University, where I held a position on the faculty. I was sitting in a living room that was beautifully decorated with dozens of red roses. My heart pounded with a mixture of happiness, pride, expectation and anxiety. Next to me sat a man who was, at that time, the only person on this earth with whom I felt completely familiar and comfortable. Or shall I say I loved him? Since I was about to get married to him, and since everything was so right and beautiful—the roses, the champagne glasses, the caviar, our hosts (Mr. and Mrs. Schiff, who were friends of my husband-to-be) and two other equally respectable couples—since everything was so right and beautiful, should I not use the word *love* rather than just familiarity? Well, in a way, I loved my husband-to-be. But I believe my love was of a different kind than the love a bride is supposed to feel just before her wedding ceremony. And while I would use the term "love" when speaking to a casual acquaintance, I do not want to deceive you, my dream reader.

The doorbell rang; it was the rabbi. Lengthy introductions, a bit of small talk and then the rabbi asked Zuzu (my dear name for my husband-to-be) and me whether we were familiar with the Jewish marriage ceremony. No, we were not, even though both of us were of Jewish descent. "Well, maybe we could use a brief rehearsal," said the rabbi, and he opened his book the wrong way, as if he wanted to read the last page first. This is the Hebrew way of writing: from what would be the back of an English book to the front of the book and from the right of the line to the left of the line. He started to read in Hebrew which I did not understand. How on earth am I going to say "I do" in Hebrew, and how will I know when to say it? Well, this turned out not to be a serious problem since Zuzu was asked first if he wanted to take me as his wife, and even though he did not understand Hebrew either, he seemed to know when to say "I do" and said it in English. I followed his example, and this part went all right. Then I was given a glass of red wine—I knew this was going to happen, so I was not too amazed, except that my hand trembled and I was afraid to spill the wine. There was another thing about the wine which I have never told anyone before. At that time I associated mostly with Christians, and when I drank the wine I had to force a thought out of my mind, a thought which seemed most heretical and sinful, namely that the wine was a symbol of Christ's blood as it is in the New Testament.

The short rehearsal which the rabbi had suggested lasted pretty long, I thought, and from a certain point on I did not know whether we were still rehearsing or whether we were already getting married. And when the ceremony was over I was still in doubt. But when we received congratulations and best wishes, I was quite sure that I was now Mrs. Joelson.

I tend to make boners at important ceremonial occasions, and I made a big one during my wedding. As Zuzu and I stood side by side still unmarried, the rabbi said to me in English, pointing towards the wedding guests: "Whom would you like to stand up with you?" He might as well have spoken Hebrew, because I didn't know what "stand up" meant. Not for a second did I connect it with a bridesmaid, since I thought that the participation of bridesmaids was limited to very formal church services. Most likely the rabbi wanted me to select someone to stand next to me in order to give me strength and support, I thought. My glance fell on Dr. Burns, who was a good friend of mine and the head of my department at the university. He was a tall and virile-looking man, a mountaineer from the Kentucky bluegrass area; if you had to pick someone to give you strength, he would be the most likely choice. But as I pointed at him, a very slight commotion went through the audience and I had the feeling that something was going on of which I was not aware. But Dr. Burns (or Burnie, as we called him), unruffled by the guests' reaction, came forward until he stood right next to me.

Later, after the wedding, Mr. Schiff said to Burnie: "You are the cutest bridesmaid I have ever seen!" And within a split second I realized what I had done. About two weeks later, the *State Psychological Association News* carried a notice of my boner with the heading ALWAYS A BRIDESMAID, NEVER A BRIDE.

And now I must tell you about Zuzu. I shall explain and I shall describe. But when doing so, I must draw a firm line of demarcation between my marriage to Zuzu and my relationship with him. First the marriage. All my life I thought I would have to get married someday, but I never expected fulfillment or happiness from being someone's wife.

Zuzu was intelligent and well educated though not an intellectual. That did not bother me, but it did bother Mother. "If only he would be a collector of rare paintings or sculptures," she said. "Do you really want to marry someone who is only an industrialist?" (Zuzu was an executive in a wood-veneer factory.) With regard to my mother's objections, I used my planned strategy and told her that I was in love. And to a certain extent this was true.

Also, some of Mother's friends commented that it was too bad that so pretty a woman as her daughter would marry a man who was not really handsome enough for her. Mother's friends were exclusively elderly Viennese women. Standards of beauty must differ from culture to culture, because American-born women found Zuzu most handsome and attractive, and sometimes I wished they would not make so much fuss about him.

Since I have no more to say about my marriage to Zuzu, let me tell you about him as a person and about my relationship with him. We became acquainted through a social worker named Alice; both Alice and I worked in what would now be called a community clinic. (At that time I worked simultaneously as a full-time teacher and a full-time clinician in order to gain experience and to make enough money to support Mother.) Alice thought we would make a good couple, perhaps because we were both foreign-born, Jewish and reasonably close in age. When we met I was thirty-four years old and he was forty-two. Zuzu was born in Riga, Latvia, and was a very distant relative of the famous jazz singer Al Jolson (whose original name was Joelson). He went to high school in Russia, studied engineering in Germany, and then worked at various industrial and commercial occupations in Paris. While he was in Germany, he married a Viennese woman named Helen. The couple fled to the United States when Hitler marched into Paris. Several years later Helen died of breast cancer, but she always remained alive in her husband's heart. Zuzu found a position in a wood-veneer factory located in Edinburgh, a town close to Indianapolis, where I lived. Thus, by way of two different itineraries we found each other, fatefully, in a city near the center of the United States.

The wedding which I described in some detail was in no way a beginning. We had already been lovers for nearly eight years before we decided to get married.

When I think of Zuzu, I most often see him coming home from work on Saturday around noon. Home was at that time a little wooden house in Edinburgh where I lived with him before we were married, every weekend from Friday to Monday. When it was time for him to come home, I used to sit down by the window and push the curtains aside so I could see him as soon as he turned the corner. When I daydream about this moment I usually let it be winter, the street covered with snow, and icicles hanging from the edges of the roofs. And here he comes. He is wearing a heavy, gray-checkered jacket, and he must be awfully cold, because the collar of his jacket is turned up so as to cover his ears. He is wearing a small brown hat pushed down over part of his forehead, and in addition to all this, he is trying to keep warm by making himself smaller—pulling up his shoulders so as to almost disappear in his shell. You'd think there is not much Zuzu to see through my window, but there is, because there is one part of him that he cannot protect by creeping into his woollen garments, and this part is his nose. The nose is big, thick and very expressive. As he approaches the house, the nose becomes more prominent, and he begins to look like a gnome—a good gnome, a sweet gnome, a funny and lovable gnome. And if you think that I am imagining all this you are wrong, because children and little dogs are immediately attracted to him and try to touch his nose and look into his twinkling eyes. (Besides being a lovable gnome, Zuzu was also Mr. Michael Joelson, a very successful industrialist, but his professional assets did not enter into my relationship with him.)

The door opens, he comes in, puts his arms around me and kisses me. His jacket is soft and a little wet and smells terrible and wonderful at the same time. The wood veneers which the factory makes have a pungent odor that gets attached to every piece of garment. It did not take too long for me to love the bad odor, because it enveloped me with tenderness.

And then Zuzu releases his embrace, clasps his hands and asks, "Hasinke, Mammusinka, comment ça va?" Now this means "Little Hare, Little Mammie, how is it going?" I don't know what language he is speaking when he says "Hasinke, Mammusinka," perhaps it is Latvian, perhaps Russian, perhaps Hebrew. Whatever language it is, it sounds like a caress and brings the warmth and earthiness of Eastern European Jews right into my heart. But I know that when he says "comment ca va?" he is speaking French, and French is a sweet language for me, too; it is the language of my childhood, since I was raised by a Swiss governess from Geneva.

The odor of wood veneer was also the scent which woke me up during vacations when I was able to stay in Edinburgh longer than just for the weekend. Zuzu had to go to work early, and just before he left he would come to my side of the double bed in his work clothes. Bending down, he would embrace me and my pillow, whispering "Fais dodo (go to sleep), Mammusinka." Enveloped in the odor which was still on his jacket from yesterday's work, I would go back to sleep with a feeling of sweetness.

My relationship with Zuzu was the first of its kind in my life. My relationship with men usually started with strong infatuations which disappeared as soon as the relation became reality. Therefore I often tried to prolong the period of infatuation; and when it finally had to come to an end, I was often left with empty hands; nothing new developed which would replace the bliss of infatuation.

My relationship with Zuzu started with the usual infatuation, but the relation became reality in an unusual manner. I was sitting in my living room in Indianapolis, where I worked and lived, waiting for him to take me out to dinner. The bell rang. I opened the door and heard him coming up the stairs. And there he was, the man who had been the object of my adoring and voluptuous fantasies for several months.

He took off his coat and, without any introduction, took me in his arms and kissed me on the mouth. This was the first kiss we had given each other. It happened again: the infatuation disappeared almost immediately, but this time something else took its place—something that, at the age of thirty-four I had never experienced before. Most men do not seem to know how to embrace a woman. They press their hard body

41

against your soft body, making it difficult to breathe by depriving your breasts of *Lebensraum.* Like a general embracing his troops before a battle, as if he wanted to say "Victory or death!" But not Zuzu. He put his arms around me with immense tenderness and gentleness, and kissed me softly at first and then a little stronger. This tenderness, a new experience for me, remained with us until the end. At that time, at the end of our marriage, there was much hatred between us, and sometimes I had nightmares about him and woke up screaming. Then he would take me in his arms and, again, I felt his tenderness and care even in the midst of separation and divorce.

Especially before we were married, we were like two frightened children who put their heads together in fear, trying to comfort each other. We were still in flight from Hitler, unable to grasp what had happened to us. There was much sadness about our friendship. I felt it often when I sat in the living room in Zuzu's house. The furniture was old, and somewhere on a small table there was a crystal bourbon set which people might have used at the beginning of this century. Everything pointed to the past, nothing to the future. We had been hurt so badly that we needed a refuge from the strain of getting used to a new world we did not understand and which did not understand us. We were so tired from our work that we needed to rest without having enough time to do so.

And yet there was something immensely sweet in this return to childhood, to our refuge from the alien world. It almost seems that we experienced something that people rarely feel when they become adults. When we were together, our adulthood disappeared with all its practicality and rationality and its adjustment to the world.

It almost seemed as if I nursed him on my breasts and he nursed me on his. And he had such a talent to say things which meant immensely more than what he said. For example, he called me "lapin blanc" (a white rabbit) and himself "lapin marron" (a brown rabbit). Once I had to go to Chicago, as an adult, as a consultant to a clinic. Therefore I could not come to Edinburgh that week. And Zuzu said: "On écrase des petits lapins blancs là-bas" (They crush little white rabbits there, in Chicago). What he meant was: don't become an adult, don't go to Chicago, don't leave me here alone in our doll house. And he further meant: don't try to shift for yourself, don't be a consultant. It is so much nicer to be a white rabbit and to stay here with your brown rabbit. But all that was condensed into one sentence.

Sometime later I asked him what he had done the night before. He replied, "I read."

"What did you read?"

"My old books."

The old books came from a small bookshelf in the den. They looked used and shabby and were mostly classics and nonfiction which he had brought from Paris. When he said "my old books" his eyes looked so very sad. Again, he was saying much more: Will I always keep reading my old books? Will I ever be able to read new books? Will I ever be able to stride into the future happily and confidently? And his doubt about the future was expressed by the fact that he never bought more than one piece of soap, or one can of tomato juice, at one time. He was not certain that the sun would rise tomorrow.

The wonderful miracle about our friendship was that we were so congenial on a feeling level. We understood each other in the land of unreality, in our dream world. And we had dozens and dozens of little sayings, little quotations which nobody listening to us could have understood in any language. A relationship of this kind was quite possible as long as the two rabbits remained by themselves without making an attempt to enter into the mainstream of society as a couple. And we did this for at least ten years.

Soon after we were married, we moved into the fairly large city of Indianapolis, which was within commuting distance from both our places of work. (At that time I was already on the faculty of Purdue's graduate school.) There we lived in an exquisitely furnished, four-room apartment. Most of the furniture was designed by Zuzu, who had considerable artistic talent. One day a woman on the editorial staff of *House Beautiful*—I have forgotten how we met her—suggested preparing an illustrated article about our apartment for her magazine. One picture was supposed to be our living room with both of us sitting on the spacious sofa. But at that time we were already somewhat uncertain about the permanence of our relationship and therefore wanted to avoid being immortalized together in *House Beautiful*.

I am sure you must have noticed that our common lifestyle had changed considerably. There was a big step from the little Hansel-and-Gretel house in the small village of Edinburgh and the city apartment which attracted the attention of *House Beautiful.* But even in the new apartment, the original flavor of our relationship remained alive for some time.

But now I cannot delay it any longer. I must tell you about the end of our relationship. When Zuzu and I became lovers and when we were married, he was a man of moderate means. But later, I believe it was in the late fifties, he became very wealthy. And I can only guess what went on within him when this happened and how it affected our relationship. Several times, usually on Sundays, he left the apartment without inviting me to go with him. He went to see friends, he said, and to look at some houses. And when he came back he used to say, "You should see how other people live!" I imagine he had visited friends or acquaintances in some of the most exclusive neighborhoods in the city, had seen their houses, their beautifully landscaped yards, their luxurious interiors and, finding himself accepted by the people in this social circle, he became eager to join them. But I was not willing and probably not able to adopt a lifestyle of this kind.

But now, Dream Reader, because we have become much closer to each other since we met on the first page of this book, I don't want to talk down to you by giving you such superficial explanations. Perhaps something much deeper had taken place. It has always been a riddle for me how a man who possesses so much warmth and tenderness can be as cruel, as selfish, and as acquisitive as Zuzu was during the last period of our common life. But one thing which he said gave me a little hint and helped me guess what might have happened to both of us. He said repeatedly, in English, the language of his rational, practical and conforming side, and also the language he spoke when he was angry with me: "Whenever I think of all this stuff like *Malchick* [I used to call him that—it means "little boy" in Russian] or white rabbit, I get sick and feel like vomiting!" At other times he referred to other childlike things that we had said or done, but all his outbursts ended with "I feel like vomiting!" Now why? He had enjoyed this childlike and playful interchange when it occurred. Why vomit now?

I think I know. There is a land in all of us in which we lived when we were children. It is all play, all sweetness, all breast to suckle and all comfort; no guilt, no shame, and no responsibility. And we had lured each other into this land; I lured him and he lured me.

Sometimes, when our adult lives become unlivable, we can go back to that land that was but is no more. But if we stay there too long, we suddenly feel the cold grip of fear: the fear of madness. Zuzu felt it, and he tore himself out of this so tempting place. He closed the trapdoor and found himself a niche in a sane and conventional world, and he hated me, the woman who brought him very close to madness. But I decided to remain in the land that was and is no more, and to go mad, because Zuzu left me alone and denied the beauty and validity of those games which I liked so much more than adulthood. Intellectually I had developed healthily and triumphed, but emotionally I am still much more childlike than most adults—for example, I wanted to buy a little E.T. doll that says "E.T. phone home" when you squeeze it, and I adore Disneyland.

We remained separated from then on, with several unsuccessful attempts to reunite. Zuzu kept in constant touch with me while I was sick. We were finally divorced in 1972.

Religion

Religion was, for me, what sex was for other children. It was secret and forbidden, and I was punished for exploring it.

When I was five, six and seven, I had a governess from Switzerland whose name was Simonette. She was a Roman Catholic of great devotion. One of her many functions was to take me for a daily walk: fresh air was viewed as "good for you." But for Simonette daily attendance of the Holy Mass was a much higher value than fresh air. Thus, she would plan our walks in such a way that we stood right in front of the cathedral (St. Stephen's Cathedral in the center of Vienna) at five o'clock. Then she shook her finger at my nose and said: "Don't you tell anybody we went to church, you hear?"

She knew my mother was opposed to church attendance, not on the ground that we were Jews, but that the air in church, saturated with incense and the odor of poor people, was not as good as the air outdoors. However, I believed the secrecy of the adventure was due to something else, something forbidden and veiled within the church, something good children should not be exposed to. And these "somethings" were always sweet and wonderful.

And they were! Even the outside of St. Stephen's was mysterious. I liked to glance at all the gargoyles looking out of holes and niches like heavenly moles. They seemed half animal and half man, and looked at me as if they meant to tell me something, something that was missing in my life.

And then we entered. It was dark, but I could see the enormous pillars which separated the central aisle from the side aisles—rising from the floor, rising up and up, followed by my glance, until they became invisible in the mist and fog of incense. No, I shall not believe what I was taught at home. I shall not believe that this church was erected by men, was gradually built between the eighth and twelfth centuries A.D., and that its style was Gothic—as contrasted to other styles like Renaissance, baroque and rococo. No, I shall not believe that the church belongs to the realm of the intellectual about which one must learn the facts without the feelings. Deep in my heart I thought that St. Stephen's was built by God just like a forest and that the pillars were trees which grew towards the firmament.

Simonette had dipped her fingers into the holy water; then she genuflected and touched her forehead, her chest and both her shoulders. Then we walked through the aisle to our pew. I looked left and right and saw mysterious niches with statues and little altars and side aisles with ornamental gates protecting precious objects. I pulled Simonette's sleeve towards these hidden treasures, but she was not to be distracted. Soon we sat in our pew. The Mass had not begun yet. Left and right of the main altar were two small altars with a statue standing on each holding out its arms as if to bless the kneeling people below. Many old women with black scarves around their heads and old men with heavy canes approached the altars, lighted a candle which seemed to come from nowhere, and put the flickering light in a red glass standing on a surface which I could not discern. The flickering candles around the left altar seemed to speak to me. "Come and see!" they said. And then the right altar joined in and said: "Come and see me, too!"

Then I felt something I could not explain, a feeling I remember having had when sitting in a rowboat with my friend Trude. The rowboat floated quietly on a small Alpine lake. The water was completely unruffled. The lake was surrounded by mountains with glaciers on top that reflected the sun. It was noon. A small Austrian village spread lazily along the shore. The church bells began to ring, and the sound created ripples on the surface of the water. Then the bells went silent and the water was smooth again. It felt as if I, as a separate being, had dissolved in all that beauty. I said to Trude, "God has touched me," and she understood.

Now in the cathedral, when the little candles flickered in red glasses, when the old people with furrowed faces knelt, moving their lips in prayer, and later when the priest said the Mass and lifted his hands to Heaven, holding something which seemed to be the key to life, I had to know, I had to know. I ran forward, up two steps, and grabbed his beautiful and bright and glittering robe, stretching my arms towards the secret in his hands to see, to touch, to feel it. I heard a murmur in the congregation and felt two arms around my waist, the arms of Simonette. She dragged me down the stairs and said, "You Jewish brat!" I did not understand. I could not tell my mother, I was afraid to speak to Trude and the other girls. Perhaps God was for others, not for me.

When I was nine, ten and eleven, a dream would come back to me night after night. I found myself in the Vienna Woods, and as I walked through a dense forest, I came to a small opening filled with magic objects. An old and wrinkled woman sat on a small chair. She was surrounded by a multitude of holy paintings—of St. Mary, and of Jesus, and of saints—showing the stories told in the New Testament. I did not understand the pictures, but I felt the holy aura which surrounded them. The paintings were loosely fastened to the stems of trees. There was much glitter from a display of beads and crosses of rosaries. Behind the scene was a little grotto where the Blessed Virgin held the Christ child. The scene looked like a shrine or like a hidden store of holy objects. Each time I awoke after dreaming, I felt sure I must have seen a place like this within the real world. I walked in all directions through the Vienna Woods. I asked passersby if they knew of a nearby grotto where souvenirs were sold. I even asked the forest ranger, and he said there was no grotto.

I did not understand then, but now I do: the grotto could not be seen by anyone but me, because it was located in the magic world within my soul. And in this magic world, we gather the notions and desires that seem as sweet to us as nectar, the notions and desires that do not fit into the world in which we live.

I had to hide the little grotto with the flickering candles. It was so much like what I saw with Simonette in the cathedral. Except for one thing: in my inner world there was no voice which said, "You Jewish brat!" And thus, it is not hard to understand that I moved my grotto and many other spiritual needs into my inner life where they were safe. And then there was another reason for this secrecy. Religion, God, and more so Jesus and the Holy Virgin—they did not fit into the modern rational, factual and scientific world, into the mildly Jewish world in which I was brought up. Later, I do not know exactly when, I closed the trapdoor to the magic world within me and became as rational and factual and

48

scientific as my home, my school and my profession demanded. The little grotto in the Vienna Woods remained imprisoned in my soul. Thus, I had been starved so many years for lack of faith and meaning, worship and surrender. And this starvation led me to a strange experience. The place was Göttingen, North Germany, where I was studying for one semester at the university. I was twenty-two years old. The year was 1932, one year before Hitler became chancellor of Germany. A Hitler rally was announced in Göttingen, and flags with swastikas covered the roofs and gables of the old university town. Out of curiosity, I went to the rally. I sat in the third row on a hard bench. The loud, marching music went through all my bones, the drums resounded in my ears, and two huge, illuminated swastikas faced the crowd. When every seat was filled, the band stopped playing marches and started to lead the crowd in German songs, the songs I learned when I was just a child during World War I. Then the many songs were crowned by the one song which drew the final spark from the electrified crowd, the German National Anthem:

Deutschland, Deutschland
Über Alles,
Über Alles in der Welt.
(Germany, Germany
Above all others
Above all others in the world.)

And then, between the two illuminated swastikas, Adolf Hitler appeared and began to speak. The only people I had ever heard speak to a crowd were high school teachers or university professors who spoke slowly, clearly, rationally and mostly without passion. I had never listened to a Baptist preacher or to an evangelic revivalist. Hitler spoke loudly and with a burning passion. His diction was full of drama and pathos. He did not mention the word *Jew* a single time. He spoke about the Treaty of Versailles, which followed World War I, when the victorious nations deprived the Germans of *Lebensraum,* of space to live, and of colonies for German industry and trade. About inflation and depression caused by the countries which were in power. And he swore he would not rest until Germany would be a nation of strength, health, and racial purity.

49

I thought I knew who Adolph Hitler was and what his Nazi Party would do to German Jews. Of course, my wildest fantasies never reached the thought that six million Jews would be put to death by poison gas. But I did know that this spectacular display of might was not for me. I knew these were my enemies. But this knowledge did not affect me in the midst of banners, flags, songs and drums, swastikas, and the thundering voice which spoke and swept me off my feet: this was my first "religious," mystical experience since Simonette took me to the Mass. And, again, an outcry against the Jews was a still unspoken part of this idolatry.

When would *my* savior come to give some meaning to *my* life? My question was answered by a dream: I am entering a church. Behind me is a man whom I know, but the dream does not reveal who he is. I open the door to the church. It is pitch-dark inside. I hear the voice of the man behind me. He says: "You must turn on *your own* light." Over the years the dream recurred again and again. Perhaps it said: you are not to join a synagogue or church. Instead, you are to create your own religion that fits your feelings and your experience of life.

Dream Reader, are you still with me? It must be that in the realm of fantasies and of delusions I tried to fulfill a wish which reality could not fulfill for me. My yearning for the spiritual and mystical pervaded my life. But each time I thought, "This is fulfillment," someone said, "No, go away, you are a Jew."

But no, Dream Reader, I have again misled you as well as myself. No other person has the power to deny spiritual fulfillment to someone who desires it. The enemy was not another person, the enemy was I. My trapdoor would not let me fulfill my need for the divine, my need for moral values, my need for meaning and purpose. I did not know what I was meant to do here on this earth and was therefore in a deep depression. In Göttingen my studies of math and physics were bland and incomprehensible to me. My first sexual relationship in Vienna at age twenty-one had seemed meaningless. I viewed myself as ugly (later that year I had my nose fixed and viewed myself as pretty. In Göttingen people told me I was beautiful). In this seeming desert (Göttingen), one thing penetrated my indifference and made me feel strongly: Hitler.

Tobey

After relationships with my husband and colleagues had been severed, I lived for more than a year in a state of loneliness and separation from my fellow beings. I was fifty-two years old. My depression was so deep that, looking at the clock, I sometimes wondered if I would be able to survive the next five minutes.

At the end of 1962, I was hospitalized for tuberculosis at Valley View, a public hospital for pulmonary diseases. Zuzu and I had been living apart for a year, and someone had told him I looked sick. He drove sixty miles from his home to where I lived and took me to a hospital, where I was diagnosed as having TB. Then I was transferred to Valley View. My physicians believed me to be very close to death. They told me that I had been dying gradually during the past years, that I had been dying in the midst of a college campus in full view of my students and colleagues.

When I first woke from deathlike sleep and found myself in the hospital, my glance fell upon the television screen. I saw figures step dancing with yellow straw hats and black canes which they juggled while they performed their dance. The scene was mute; there was no sound that I could hear. I thought, "There still are people dancing somewhere. There is a world outside that has not yet been destroyed. No A-bomb fell, no world disaster. It is I who died, but not the world."

Once I called a nurse and asked her to send a telegram to my grandparents saying THE GREENERY IS STILL ALIVE. My grandparents died before I was born. It seemed almost as if I had been in another world where I could communicate with the dead—as if I wanted to tell my grandparents that I was not ready yet to join them.

51

During that time I had a recurrent dream which came not only during deep sleep but also during the twilight zone between sleeping and waking. In this dream I found myself weightlessly suspended inside a long, black, vertical shaft. The shaft was made of heavy black canvas; its cross section seemed to be a quadrangle measuring about one square yard. The canvas was supported by squares made of pine sticks distanced about six feet apart. I floated within the canvas, moving very slowly upwards. The canvas was so long that I could see neither its end nor its beginning. The similarity of my dream to the reports of Drs. Kübler-Ross and Moody about the images of persons who were falsely pronounced dead is striking. Maybe I never saw the end of the shaft because death was not yet ready to receive me.

All these fantasies seemed very strange to me, and thus I decided to record them in a diary. At first it was an enormous effort. I wrote with both my head and the pad of paper resting on the pillow:

I am so very isolated from the rest of the world. Not too long ago my physicians viewed me as being very close to death. I have to lie in bed for twenty-four hours a day, in a single room attended by nurses and physicians who wear surgical masks so that only their eyes are visible.

Yesterday my physician told me that I must not write until I am further along on the path of recovery.

At last, after two months, the day has come when I can write again.

Now I am permitted to sit in a chair and to look out of the window. And my depression has gradually yielded to a feeling of peace and contentment. Contemplation is my main occupation in the hospital. Looking out into the yard, I see trees and the sky and the change of colors as the clock moves from morning to night. I see nurses and doctors hurrying from building to building as if they were not aware of the golden beauty of nature around them. And I see patients strolling on the narrow pathways, talking and laughing as they go along. Ah, sweet adversity!

> *The evening is my favorite time. The sun has gone down behind the hills, but the sky is still light. The noise of the day has died down, and the busy world is hushed. A dog is barking in the distance. The fever of life is over, there is peace at last. Outside a lonely lunger (patient with lung disease) sits on a bench slowly blowing the smoke from his pipe skywards. My heart is at rest.*

After having been in the tuberculosis hospital for a time span that seemed like years, but must have been only several weeks, someone very important came into my life. He was so tiny, so light, so blond, and so pale that he almost merged into the background. He was everything and yet nothing. He was frightened and pleading at times, bold and manly at others. And often he was coy and impish. His name was Tobey. Tobey Godsey. He was four years old.

> *There is a room across the hall, big, square, and empty. An iron bed, a nightstand, a rusty steel locker. The room seems gray and misty. But today I look and I see it is different. A little boy is standing there. He looks almost transparent. He wears dark-blue corduroy trousers and a striped T-shirt. His arms hang listlessly at his sides. He holds a rag doll in his right hand. The doll, too, is hanging down listlessly. It is as if the listless doll is a replica of the listless little fellow.*
>
> *I ask, "What is your name?" He looks through me as if I were invisible. I wish there was despair on his face or sadness, but there is not. Just emptiness. He is alone in a big cold room of steel. He*

*has never been alone before, always with his
mother or father. Now he is sick; his left lung has
collapsed and he has TB. Now he is alone.*

It lasted about two weeks. Two weeks of aloneness with a listless
raggedy doll. Two weeks of staring into space. Two weeks of "What's
your name?" And two weeks without reply.

*Today it happened. The little fellow received
a haircut. It makes him look like a little man.
Maybe he likes that, for when he comes back from
the barber and passes by my door, he emerges for
a split second from behind the yellow uniform of
the nurse, turns around with incredible speed like
a spinning top, and then rushes back into hiding.
I suspect he is proud of his haircut; I suspect he
wanted to show it to me.*

After the day when we first make contact, Tobey is different. I wake
up in the morning. The terror is incredible. Looking around the room,
I see the bare windows, the steel bed; there is the realization that
everything has gone, everything I worked for all my life. Then the door
opens: a nurse dressed in yellow with a breakfast tray; and behind her,
the little fellow. Only his head emerges, and the upper part of his body
is bent forward. His face wears an expression I have never seen before.
I search for words to describe that wonderful little face that can express
everything there is in the world. The eyes are eager, sparkling. He must
have been awake for a long time. And then there is something I cannot
describe; he looks as if he has something up his sleeve. I listen and he
calls: "Peekaboo, I see you." And I reply, drowsily and half-asleep,
"Peekaboo, I see *you.*"

From here on there is an agreement between us, an agreement
without words: it's you and me together; we shall overcome loneliness.

My door is often closed when I am too sick to bear the noise in the
hall. But the man who cleans the floors tells me about the little fellow.
"What's your name?" the little fellow has asked him. And then, "Will

you do me a favor?" We laugh about Tobey using words like an adult. The man tells me that then the little fellow looked at him pleadingly and said, "Open dat door," and while he said it he eagerly bent forward with his legs akimbo and pointed to my door. The man says he told Tobey that I was asleep, and Tobey replied, "That's all right. I'll wake her up." The little fellow likes me. I have a friend.

Now I'd like to tell you of all the things that happened between Tobey and me.

I soon find out that I am to follow Tobey's lead, for he seems strong and full of ideas. He wants to tell me how we should plan our day.

For example, one day he stands on his sidewalk again as he so often does. That is, the white stripe that runs along the side of the hall in front of his door. It is the rule of the hospital that he may not go beyond the stripe in order to come close to my door, for our disease is catching. He looks up at me as if he wants to intrigue me, as if to tell me that something is about to begin. Then he jumps up a tiny bit and down again on his feet so as to stand with his little shoes apart, his knees slightly curved, and his body bent forward eagerly. Then he looks up at me with a smile and a challenge and asks: "Dis one?"

I am intrigued, as he intended, and then I nod as I always do, even when I don't understand. Then he repeats the act, this time landing slightly closer to me on his sidewalk. He asks, "Dat one?" and comes still closer to me on the sidewalk. "Dis one?" and then, "Dat one?" By this time his face has an almost devilish expression as he looks at me with a sparkle in his eyes. I look at Tobey's feet and understand. They are both planted firmly on the blue linoleum outside his white sidewalk. "Dis one?" and I rule firmly, "No."

We play the game many times, and as always when I watch Tobey, I feel a strange fascination, though I can only guess the significance of what he is doing. Maybe he is testing the limits of what I will permit him to do. I try to partake in his game to the best of my knowledge. As he jumps down within his limits, I nod as if to say yes. And when he jumps so that his little toes exceed the line by only half an inch or so and he looks up with his teasing eyes, I wait; then I say, "Yes." When a good part of his foot is beyond the sidewalk, I say, "No," using the best of my judgment. But when he altogether jumps off his sidewalk, I shake my head firmly and strongly, often with fear. That is the game the way we like to play it.

Sometimes the game ends differently: some kind of inebriation seems to seize the little fellow at any point in his act. Then he jumps forward and backward with incredible speed, not heeding limits or sidewalk, in a crooked zigzag line that leads back to his room, and throwing his head from left to right and from right to left, he shouts gaily: "Dis one, dat one, dis one, dat one, dis one, dat one . . . "

Dream Reader, you might wonder, Why does this adult woman tell us about the games she played with a four-year-old? There is nothing unusual about these games. Maybe you would add: my Johnny did things like this all the time.

Well, you see, I never had a Johnny or a Joan. I occasionally played with children of relatives or friends; I also conducted a part-time nursery school for three years, but I never had one of these imps all to myself twenty-four hours a day. I became, in part, his fictitious mother. He once said indignantly: "Why don't you get up? My mommy doesn't lie in bed all day." But I was a mother without any responsibilities. The hospital personnel fed him, kept him clean and restored his health. All I had to do was enjoy him.

I was in part mother, in part peer. My illness, my total dependency, and the fact that I was unable to engage in any adult activities made a four-year-old out of me: not unlike Tobey, it was my main concern to fill the time with childlike activities. Tobey was even ahead of me: he urinated and defecated into his potty without the help of a nurse, while I had to be given a bed pan, since I was not permitted to leave my bed. He had won the competition between us. He was triumphant that he was more mature concerning toilet training, since a bed pan was for him like using diapers.

Tobey is with me during the arduous beginning; he is with me when I start to rebuild the world. He spends much time sitting on his narrow bed with one little leg hanging down over the edge, but not quite touching the floor, and the other leg folded under his body so that he is almost sitting on it. His eyes are turned towards the television screen, and he

56

seems to watch it. He leaves me alone, but when my terror becomes too strong, I know how to call him. It sounds like "hee-hee," and when the little fellow hears it, he jumps off his bed, storms to his post in front of the door, eager, sparkling, and full of adventure.

But then there are other times when the little fellow needs me, and I leave him alone. I am dazed and drowsy. Then he calls me. But his way of calling is different from mine. He bends forward and says something that sounds like "Wing-wing-wing-wing-wing, your phone is ringing." But I am as if in a stupor. I do not hear him. And then he bends forward and calls again, "Wing-wing-wing-wing, your phone is ringing." This time louder, slower and with painful insistence, as if talking to someone who is deaf or dumb. My phone is on the nightstand. It is not ringing. But I understand Tobey's message.

There are other times when my door is closed. Then I hear a little voice calling with the same intense deliberation. "Me twist, me twist!" He knows I like to see him twist (dance); he wants me to open the door.

Tobey knows that he has been sick, but he does not know that he is still sick, and he objects whenever I mention it to him. "You sick, me well," he declares, and I smile.

As time goes on, we become more and more dependent on each other, and now the little fellow wants to have me all for himself. When I tell him my husband is coming to visit, he sulks and says angrily, "Tell 'im we don't need 'im!"

Unfortunately I am unable to assuage the pain which Tobey feels whenever I pay the slightest attention to anyone else but him. I tend to tape the humorous get-well cards which I receive daily from my husband on the wall over my bed. Whenever Tobey sees me do this, he tears a page out of his paint book and writes on it in large block letters TOBEY. Then he skips into the hall until his toes touch the edge of the sidewalk, bends forward, stretches his arms as far as they will reach, the sheet in his hands, and requests, "Hang dat up." The little fellow wants to be remembered, and so my wall is covered with reminders saying TOBEY TOBEY TOBEY TOBEY TOBEY.

♥

Soon it becomes clear to me that the affection Tobey and I feel for each other is strongly approved by Tobey's mother, while his father is afraid that our friendship might breed contagion and add to Tobey's illness, even though we never come close to each other. The chewing

57

gum which I buy for Tobey several times a week has to be given to a nurse, who unwraps it and then passes it on to Tobey. However, Tobey's father does not approve even of this highly careful procedure. (A fact which I do not know at the time.)

This exchange of chewing gum leads to many funny incidents. When Tobey knows that some gum is in my possession, he shouts impatiently, "*Me* want your gum!" Apparently my illness has not destroyed my teacherly inclinations, so I correct: "Tobey, *I* want your gum." Whereto Tobey replies, first whining and then stamping his foot, "*You* want *my* gum? No, *I* want *your* gum." And since we need a nurse to unwrap the gum, he screams with a marked German accent which he only could have acquired from me, "Nös, nös, nös!" And after he finally gets to chew his goodie, he turns to the nurse and says with an angelic smile, "Thank you."

"You should thank Dr. Joelson," replies the nurse. "She gave you the gum." However, Tobey looks at the nurse and again says, "Thank you" to *her*. This little act is usually repeated several times.

First I felt rejected, but now I understand the little fellow's strategy. He pretends not to understand that I was the giver of the gum, since his father does not permit any interaction between us. I feel proud of Tobey's intelligence and am sure that his IQ is at least 150. And my brain—so very restless and hungry for new stimulation—starts to make plans to send Tobey to college, and then, who knows? Maybe a degree in diplomatic science.

While writing all this I cannot help repeating that the little events which I experience in the tuberculosis hospital are in no way unusual or dramatic in the eyes of others, but they are so for me. My "rebirth" makes me see the world around me in a different light, in an altered state of consciousness. Nothing seems trivial and unimportant. Everything seems as if I am seeing it for the first time. Every person, every event, every detail seems wondrous and of great significance. Could it be that the significance which we attribute to an experience is related to our life space in such a manner that in a small life space even a small experience assumes great importance? For example, Sarah (a patient), who is a fifty-year-old factory worker and Jehovah's Witness, seems to me the most marvelous, spiritual, loving person. On the other hand, Bob, who is a young lawyer and the only other university-educated patient, seems abnormally materialistic, and I feel it is my duty to "save" him—to make him as idealistic as I am and to help him believe in God. Social injustices about which I have always known now seem unbearable.

Lately I have observed that Dr. Clark comes to see Tobey and stays in his room with the door closed for sometimes as long as half an hour, which is very rare in this hospital. I worry that the little fellow's recovery might not be proceeding as expected. First I ask Tobey about his conversations with Dr. Clark, then I speak to his mother on the phone and finally with Dr. Clark himself. No, the trouble is not Tobey's recovery at all, which, thank God, is proceeding quite well. The difficulty is based on the fact that Dr. Clark and Tobey differ radically with regard to their basic philosophy of medicine. Dr. Clark's philosophy is predominantly somatogenic: *he* believes that pulmonary tuberculosis is caused by bacteria attacking the lung tissue. In contrast, Tobey's theory is psychogenic: *he* holds that the disease is not to be found in the body but in the psyche. He is convinced that he and I would have been well and at home long ago if only he had gotten permission to bring his dog, Pudgy, with him.

"But Pudgy would run around in the hall and go into Dr. Joelson's room, into the nurses' station, and into the kitchen and would carry the little animals [bacteria], which make you sick, all over the floor," Dr. Clark says. Tobey is altogether unimpressed by little animals that can't be seen. He is more impressed by the sad and empty faces of patients, aides, and physicans, and he is convinced that happiness would prevail in the ward through the presence of the creature whom he loves more than anybody on this earth. He is sure that a small, brown dog named Pudgy could cure all of us much more quickly than the medical profession.

I have tried so long to postpone the end. I have savored every moment of writing about Tobey, but now I believe I have told you all you have to know and I must tell you about the end.

Each morning I take my daily walk, up the hall and down the hall, slowly and painfully, with my body bent forward and my knees prone to give way. And when I come back to my room, the little fellow always stands on his sidewalk with his legs akimbo and talks much and with great speed. Often I cannot understand what he says, but I nod while he speaks. And we like to be together.

But today when I return from my walk, I look and see two nurses. Then I see Tobey. But Tobey is different. He does not wear his light-blue sleepers, and his gun in his holster; nor does he wear his blue trousers and little striped shirt. Instead he is dressed to go out of the building. He wears a brown coat that is made of leather and a cap on his head that covers his ears. And when I see him I feel betrayed. We have been together to build our own little world. And now he is dressed like a boy from the outside.

I come closer to him and ask, "Tobey, where are you going?"

"I am going to another hospital. Are you coming?"

"No."

And then I say, "I shall miss you." He gives me a forced little smile. Our faces are pale, our lips are dry, and we are not able to speak. And then the tears start rolling over my cheeks.

The next day, while I am waking up, I have a new insight: I have often wondered why Tobey's mother has repeatedly said to me, "Tobey is not an ordinary boy." And now I suddenly understand. The name of the little boy who saved my life is Godsey, meaning God's Eye. It is unbelievable!

I have neglected my diary for a long time, but today there is something important to write. I am taking my first walk outdoors. I have spent eight months in my room. The time has passed quickly, and now the doctor says I may go out.

Valley View, my place of rebirth! Valley View, my home! The sun is high, the air is fresh. It is May. I look around. I am back in the world. I take a few steps and then a few more. And then I look. I look at the grass, the trees, the sky. I hear the voices of children far away.

Then I see the bird. It is sitting on an evergreen tree singing. It lifts its head and the song becomes louder. Then it seems to lift its head more and more until its beak is pointing right up to heaven. The bark of the tree seems to glow in its brownness. The evergreens are greener than I have ever seen them, and the sky is brighter. The bird's song becomes louder and louder until it sounds like jubilation. And then the whole world turns around me until it becomes a great symphony jubilating to heaven, "I am alive; I am alive."

Much later, I visit the children's ward almost daily during my walks. It is located in a separate building. I am not permitted to go into the house, but I can talk to the children through the windows or through the fence around the playground. I make an observation which interests me greatly: the children, most of whom are between three and five years old, treat me as if I were a child! For example, when it begins to get dark in the evening, the oldest one, Steve, will say: "It is getting dark, she has to go home now."

This comment starts a heated discussion, since some of the children think I could stay a little longer, the hospital being located right across the lawn, while others suggest that I should leave immediately. But none of them ever consults *me* regarding my departure.

Similarly, Joey, a four-year-old boy, asks: "Why does your mommy and daddy never come to see you?"

"My mommy is dead, Joey."

I have hardly finished the sentence, when Scottie blurts out, "Who killed her?" He is an ardent viewer of Western movies.

Joey cuts in, asking, "Where is your daddy?"

"My daddy is dead also, Joey."

"When did he die?"

"He died a long, long time ago."

Shirley wants to know more. "Where is your daddy buried?"

"Far, far away."

A pause, and then Joey's voice comes out of the window slowly and dreamily, as if he were about to fall asleep. "Dr. Joelson, is your daddy Jesus?"

The Experiment

I often wonder why my life, which has been so full of despair, has gradually become so peaceful. While I ascribe this change to a higher power, the question still remains why this power has chosen to enter my life at this particular moment. I have hit the bottom and have given up. I know from my readings about the lives of the saints that God often enters the hearts of women and men at such times.

But I am also convinced that the absence of work has freed my mind from a ballast of thoughts and has given God a chance to enter it. Now I am in this world but no longer of this world.

After years of activity and striving, I am finally able to empty my heart, my soul, my brain, to wait and see where my ship will go if I abandon the steering wheel, if I surrender to nothingness. Now I understand what Lao-tse said in praise of nothingness:

> *Thirty spokes unite in one nave,*
> *And because of the part where nothing exists*
> *   we have the use of a carriage wheel.*
> *Clay is molded into vessels,*
> *And because of the space where nothing exists*
> *   we are able to use them as vessels.*
> *Doors and windows are cut out in the walls of*
> *   a house,*
> *And because they are empty spaces, we are able*
> *   to use them.*
> *Therefore, on the one hand we have the benefit*
> *   of existence, and on the other of non-existence.*

I am happy. My life has become meaningful. I feel the presence of God as a guide. I know what I must do even though I cannot formulate it in words. At every point of decision I am certain which way to turn. I see my role as being a secular minister in academia. My students and my colleagues have seen me in this way, although the latter do not always approve of this role. I have had a *great* influence on *many* of my students.

I often ask myself why I never pray. While I feel God speaks to me in silence, I would view it as presumptuous to speak to God. It would appear especially presumptuous to ask God for favors. He knows my wishes without my telling Him, and He will fulfill them if it is His will. My heart is open and God gives. I often wonder whether Jesus was right when He said giving is sweeter than receiving. But to question Jesus' words seems sacrilegious and terribly impertinent.

My thoughts often wander to God, and for the first time in my life I feel in touch with Him. I feel as if my whole life was but a prelude to this encounter. His hand touches mine in gentle guidance, and He says, "It is I."

A few days ago I asked the librarian to bring me some how-to books on taking the cure from tuberculosis. Today she brought the books. Most of them are written by physicians or ex-patients. I thumb through all of them. The fact is stressed that a long stay in the hospital gives the patients an opportunity to better themselves—to read good literature, to take correspondence courses, to learn a craft. But nowhere do I see it mentioned that the long span of recovery is an opportunity for contemplation and that contemplation may enrich the patient's inner life. "Don't brood" is the message most books have to give. But brooding is what saved me from perdition.

I think the other patients lead lives similar to my own; they, too, are removed from the pressures and obligations of a complex society. And I feel sure that this distancing has produced insights in us which are far superior to the insights we would have had, had we remained healthy. I am certain that God has entered the other patients' lives as He has entered mine.

In my fantasy I gradually, step by step, transform the hospital into a cloister. I believe that the people who have been cured of tuberculosis are among the chosen ones and that it is their duty to go out and preach to the world what they have learned at the tuberculosis hospital—to preach a contemplative way of life, a life of listening and feeling rather than a life of moving and achieving.

It is beautiful. My thoughts give me a feeling of exhilaration, like the feeling people have when they are standing on a very high mountain. Only rarely, in the evening, when the records and the television sets are turned on high, I have the painful thought that things are not quite what they appear to be. But the thought disappears after a few moments. It does so in the beginning, anyway. But as time goes on, there are more and more dissonances in my life, things which do not rhyme and which I cannot explain.

Starting today I am permitted to mingle with other patients at mealtime. I find myself among a group of people with backgrounds very different from my own. Most of the patients have lived in the slums before they were hospitalized and, in all probability, will return to the slums after leaving the hospital. Some are illiterates, prostitutes, and ex-convicts. I assume that poverty, malnutrition and neglect have caused their disease in most cases.

I find it difficult to understand my fellow patients. They hold beliefs and values different from mine, and many of them speak with unfamiliar accents. It is especially baffling that they seek my company with such eagerness, even though it is difficult to communicate with me because I am so weak that listening, let alone responding, takes a considerable effort. What possible pleasure can my fellow patients derive from spending so much time with me? Thus, I find it difficult to understand what's going on around me.

I still don't understand why many patients seem to be unusually friendly towards me. Establishing human contact is a joyful experience because I have been alone for so long. Especially the children seem to like me.

Today is a real strange day for me. Bob, a young teacher, and I are eating lunch together. He makes me feel depressed. Our conversation is more concrete than usual. Bob is telling me about another patient, Mr. McHugh, who worries whether he will ever be able to make a living, since he gets out of breath when delivering newspapers at the sanatorium. It is not compassion for Mr. McHugh which depresses me, it is something else. Bob's tale does not seem genuine. It is as if he were not interested in what he is telling me. It is just a little thing.

Moreover, today Bob does not respond to my comment on a book by Camus. It is rather surprising since, in the past, he has always participated in our philosophical discussions with great eagerness. But today he talks about knitting, and he dwells at length on the fact that hand-knitted sweaters are more durable than machine-knitted ones. I start to feel that I don't understand what is going on around me.

As Christmas draws closer, there are more and more riddles which I cannot solve. The patients at Valley View, as in every hospital of this kind, keep busy at what is called occupational therapy. They knit, embroider, weave, make leather goods, and work with wood. But not I. I think, and I write my diary. Today I notice again that more and more patients approach me and speak to me. But what they talk about is always their occupational therapy. And they describe in great detail the objects they are making. Yet they know my thoughts are far away from such matters.

Here is a riddle. Why do they do this? Perhaps they like me and reveal to me what fills their minds rather than mine. Or perhaps their tales are hints that I, too, should be busy making things. For days and days I wonder and I listen to wool, cotton, wood, and leather.

"You have a pretty purse," says one patient.

"It is a present."

"Oh, a leather present!"

What does he mean? Then he starts to tell me what beautiful things he has made out of leather.

When one of them talks to me too long, another one pushes him away and makes his work seem even more beautiful. Oh, I suddenly understand! The people who are telling me about the goods they make are trying to sell them to me. Christmas is drawing close and everyone needs money.

Now something strange happens to me. Within a fraction of a second, my picture of Valley View and what I have experienced here reverses itself completely, like a picture seen through a kaleidoscope. This is not a cloister, not a place where people find God through leisure and contemplation. Instead it is a rat race where everyone works as hard as he can trying to make a buck, and every little merchant keeps a jealous eye on his neighbors, attempting to spoil their business in order to advance his own.

I cannot eat and I cannot sleep. I cannot speak and I cannot listen. I think of all that has happened at the sanatorium, but now I see it in a new light. And minute by minute I have new insights. In this hospital it is forbidden to solicit customers for one's wares; thus, the patients have to drop hints regarding their salable goods. And Bob, since he speaks more to me than anyone else, must have been briefed by the others to describe their work to me in the most glowing terms.

Then there is Irma, another patient. Her husband was shot by his brother. It happened a few months ago. A patient whose name I don't know told me Irma had hallucinations. She saw her dead husband sitting by her bed. I wanted to go and comfort her. I found her standing in the hall in front of her room.

"Rats! They are after me! Rats!" she yelled and pointed.

But where she pointed to I saw no rats.

I walked into her room, asked her to get into bed, and then sat down and held her hand. She is contagious, but it did not matter to me at that time.

But now a suspicion arises within me. Did she really see her dead husband? Did she see rats? Did she have hallucinations? She is poor because she has not been able to earn any money since the onset of her consumption. She knows that I am a psychologist. Perhaps she is seeking my friendship by faking hallucinations so I will give her money. Because, you see, I am the only person in the hospital who has money. I have developed a warm tenderness toward this woman. When she is upset, she permits no one to come to her room but me. But now it seems as if the wool has been pulled over my eyes.

Today another thing has happened which fits in with my interpretation. Irma says: "When I speak to you I feel like a person." Suddenly the ice in my veins melts, and I feel the warm blood streaming through my body. But later I speak to a friend of mine, a social worker, who has come to visit. She says, "People from the lower classes frequently say things like 'You make me feel like a person' to professional workers when they can use them to their advantage. They have learned to use and abuse the language which will impress the professionals." Tears roll over my cheeks when I think of the possibility that my affection has been aroused by subterfuge.

♥

Gradually I remember one incident after another which could be viewed as a commercial promotion rather than as a genuine act of friendship. It seems I am perceived as a prospective buyer or donor of money rather than as a person. Now I can interpret every incident, including the smallest detail, according to my new insight.

Take, for example, Tobey. Why did he hold up his stuffed animals to me when he saw me standing on the balcony? I thought it was to proudly show me his possessions or to induce me to love the little animals, giving them the affection which was really meant for him. But now I think he may have approached me for different reasons. Some time ago I bought two bunnies from his mother; she had made the little animals herself from bits of cotton and wool, and after that she must have taught Tobey to show me other animals so I would buy them. In my darkest moments, I believe that the little fellow's mother taught him to approach me because she knew that I could be of financial help, and that all the love he showed me was not sincere but just pretended. But now I remember how his face lit up each time I opened my door to see him. The eagerness of his little face was genuine.

Next I remember the incident of hair washing. A beautician from the neighborhood comes to see me every week to wash and set my hair. I pay her four dollars for her work. I am the only one in the hospital who engages in such luxury. Recently I observed something peculiar. Every time I went to the bathroom, there were several other women who followed me. It was quite clear that they came to the bathroom at that special moment so I could see them. They all had pink curlers in their hair. No doubt they wanted to show me that they could set their own hair, and thus they could set mine and make some money.

Several days later something even more striking happened. While I was eating breakfast in my room in the early morning, I heard a loud noise. I opened the door to the hall, and it was immediately apparent what had caused the noise. A nurse's aide had dropped a tray of dishes and silver right in front of my door. It could not have been an accident; she had done it in order to get my attention. Then I looked out and saw Mary Anne, my thirteen-year-old neighbor, setting the hair of Anabel, her fourteen-year-old roommate. She was almost finished, and the aide—turning toward me and pointing to Anabel—asked, "Doesn't she look sweet?" I immediately understood the message. They wanted to show me that Mary Anne could set someone else's hair. This, then, should persuade me to ask her to set mine.

Now that I understand that people have been trying to offer me their services, many other things fall into place. For example, Sarah, the fifty-year-old factory worker, often mentioned during meals that she had spent the morning washing. She would elaborate in great detail how she had washed and ironed one blouse and then another one, one slip and then another. I now know this was a hint, but at first I was in doubt about what she was trying to convey. Perhaps, I thought, she wanted to induce me to do my washing, too. I noticed with some embarrassment the spots on my blouse and skirt. But now I understand her hints. It was she who wanted to do my washing in order to make some extra money. Maybe she even wanted to become my maid after we both got well. At the same time, I understand why Mr. Bailey told me how well he could repair plumbing, even though he has never been trained to be a plumber.

Sometime after my discovery, one of Sarah's moving talks on Christian virtue led to her offering me a subscription to the *Watchtower*. I found her insincerity harder and harder to take. One day I wrote to my friend Rebecca that Sarah was of great spiritual beauty, and the next day I no longer felt it was true.

Before I became sick, I often read that the process of selling and buying, and of competing in doing so—the process of being friendly to people because they could become potential customers—makes genuine relationships impossible. I had never truly experienced that this was correct. But now I know it is true! What happens in the large and complex world is reflected on a small scale in our hospital. Now it is simple enough to be truly understood.

Dr. Clark told me that I can leave the hospital for a few hours every week. Last night, a freezing winter night, I returned from my short leave dressed in a warm fur coat. When we arrived at the front door of the hospital in the Cadillac my husband was driving, there were four figures there: two men and two women, looking like shadows in the dusk. Their coats were threadbare, and they were shivering in the icy wind. Was it chance, or had they gathered there so the rich could see the poor and wince in shame?

Now all my suspicions are confirmed. After the evening meal, people suddenly behave strangely toward me. Usually after dinner I ride upstairs by elevator all by myself, because the other patients prefer to take the stairs. Today, however, everything is different. Bob opens the door to the elevator for me; this time it is crowded with patients. They all are from another ward, but they ask me to come to their ward and visit. I find myself talked to, shoved and pushed, taken by the arm, and finally, almost against my will, sitting alone with Sarah, an elderly patient, in her room. She tells me how poor Irma is. (Irma is the woman who said that I made her feel like a person.) Irma's brother and sister and niece were all stricken by tuberculosis at the same time, and her husband was shot by his brother. Then she tells me about herself, that she is alone and an old woman. She does not need too much. She asks me if I could lend her ten dollars. She could return the money later, when she receives her welfare check.

I lend and give and buy. But it is hard to decide how much sharing is reasonable. For how can one person rectify the abysmal injustice of our social system? Now I suspect even more than before that Irma's hallucinations were a fake. And so was perhaps much of what has happened between me and other patients. I have developed a genuine affection for some, but they see me only as a source of money. I have to give up my image of a cloister where everyone lives in his cell quietly contemplating God. But now it no longer matters, since I believe I am about to make another exciting discovery.

It started with my medication. I have been taking the same kind and the same dose for many weeks. But yesterday, when the medication nurse came in bringing the usual brown powder and pink capsule, something had been added: a large, white pill. I asked what it was, but I did not get an answer. The same pill was added to my medication at noon and after supper. Otherwise, the day was uneventful and so was the following night.

But when I woke up this morning, everything had changed. First came the noise. On past mornings it had been quiet in my room, and all I could hear was the hum of the air-conditioner. But now there is screaming and shouting. I open the door to see who is making the noise. I find it is almost everybody. The nurses' aides scream their breakfast orders to the kitchen maid, and the kitchen maid screams back. Only yesterday the patients remained quietly in their rooms, but this morning they are all standing at the door and shouting at each other excitedly. They even look different. My young neighbor Mary Anne, for example, used to wear well-pressed, light cotton dresses and to keep her hair neat by braiding it left and right. I had often wondered about her dresses—how she kept them so clean and well ironed—and why a girl her age would not wear more informal clothes which would not require so much care. Today, for the first time, she wears blue jeans and a dirty, white T-shirt. Her hair looks uncombed—like the hair of a savage. And the other patients, too, look ungroomed, dirty, and somewhat wild.

The strangest thing of all is that even the trains which pass on the nearby railroad track seem louder. Oh now I understand. My mind catches on and I start to think sharply. It cannot be that the trains are louder today than they have been for weeks before. The change must be in me. Within a split second I venture an explanation: the white pills. I started to take them twenty-four hours ago, three yesterday and one this morning.

The thought brings vague associations to my mind and veiled hints which were made here and there. One patient said, "I was ready to go home six months ago, but they just keep us here indefinitely. All we are is guinea pigs." Guinea pigs? What did she mean?

Another time, Mrs. Godsey (Tobey's mother) said to me, "Why are you still here? I would take this up with Dr. Clark if I were you." It sounded as if she thought I was being retained at the hospital without justification. It even sounded as if she knew the reason. And again I feel that there is something which everbody knows except myself.

I begin to suspect that the tuberculosis hospital is not what it appears to be. Instead it is a place where they conduct experiments on the effect of drugs on people's thinking and behavior. Not of tuberculosis drugs, but of drugs like opium and LSD.

On the morning that I found everybody wild and loud and different, it must have been the day when everybody's medication was changed.

From my memory and from the notes in my journal, I am convinced that there has been a change of drugs every Wednesday.

My discovery makes me exhilarated and happy. At last I understand what is going on around me. But since I am not sure my discovery is correct, I shall keep it to myself, and I shall be very cautious when I speak to other people. I drop a few hints, but never state clearly what I think.

Ever since Aldous Huxley published *The Doors of Perception,* which illustrates the effect of psychedelic drugs, it has been my ardent wish to take part in an experiment on drug effects. Now my wish has been fulfilled: I shall look within me with great curiosity and expectation and note every thought and feeling.

At the same time, I feel manipulated by Dr. Clark, who is using me for his purpose without asking permission. I remember a science-fiction story in which a group of scientists keeps creatures from another planet captive in order to observe and study them. The creatures finally escape and return to their own planet. Shall I escape?

Occasionally I feel strong hatred against Dr. Clark for what he is doing to me. I assume he feels justified in doing whatever he wants with me because he saved my life. Many other patients feel this same hatred, and now I know it is the drug experiment which has given rise to it. "If I could get my hands on his throat . . . ," one patient said to me some time ago. And Bob made some furtive hint about a lawsuit for medical malpractice. Are we all prisoners?

My husband, too, has controlled me, and at times I hate him for it. For I suspect he signed an official permission that I could be used in the experiment. He has the legal right to do so—he has held the power of attorney over me since I got tuberculosis.

I was proud of all the thoughts which I had written down in my daily journal. It hurt my pride when I found out they had been induced through drugs. But if everyone reacts differently to the same drug, it is still I who thinks and not the drug. There is no one on the ward who sits and thinks and writes as I do.

But then there is God, the God whose guidance I feel so gently. Could it be a chemical God? Could my feelings of nearness and of faith be caused by drugs? I do not know. The thought that my own religious feelings—so recently developed, so tender and delicate, so easy to destroy, and so ardently needed—that these religious feelings could be induced by drugs seems shattering. I quickly invoke a dear memory, the memory

71

of a private conversation with the late theologian Paul Tillich, who affirmed that religious thoughts come from the depth of the thinker's soul and that drugs could only contribute to the thinker's becoming aware of and sharing her feelings about God. He also reminded me that one and the same drug could produce religious feelings in one person and violent acts in another.

The people on the ward are becoming wilder and wilder. I am afraid they will come into my room and tear up my journal. Perhaps this is a reason to escape. No. If I can find a safe place for my manuscript, I will stay; I shall send it to my husband, and I shall stay.

From looking at my fellow patients, there is no doubt that some of them are taking drugs different from the ones I am taking. But others are taking the same. It becomes clear to me that the people to whom I feel close, with whom I can converse with ease, who share my sense of humor and who understand me even if my words are full of hints and slight allusions, that these people are taking the same drug as I. Take Bob, for example. When something is said between us, I often do not know if it is he or I who says it. We are congenial. I think he must be taking the same drug as I am. For instance, Bob asked me at dinner time, "Is there a Dr. Miller?" (Dr. Miller is the medical director of the hospital and also my physician. I understood what he meant. No one except me ever sees him, but his signature is under all the "Do this" or "Don't do this" communications brought to us by the aides. Bob wondered, with tongue in cheek, if Dr. Miller is an invented authority figure (like God, in Bob's view). I represented idealism, which Bob denied in himself; and he represented cynicism, which I denied in myself.

The experiment must have a wider scope than just our hospital, because there are people outside with whom I have some kind of understanding. One is my husband. He, too, is taking the same drug as I.

But Rebecca, my young friend and student who visits me every week, is taking different drugs or none at all. For I can never quite get the point of what she says to me.

Irma is on my drug, no doubt.

Then there is Shirley. She called me long-distance last night. She spoke fast and with great excitement about an invention she had made to teach arithmetic to preschool children. She spoke as if her invention were the greatest thing that had happened to this earth. Yack, yack, yack for half an hour and then goodbye. No questions about me. She must have taken dope, a different one from mine.

But Conrad—a tall, slender lunger with whom I can joke like nobody's business—is on my drug. I feel sure about that.

My notion that it was leisure and contemplation which made many patients so sensitive and full of humor collapses right on my lap, and I feel sad. The chemical origin of behavior does not appeal to me.

While staying at the tuberculosis hospital, I have written a few articles and have published them in several journals. Maybe they, too, have been conceived under the influence of drugs. Some of my colleagues have written me complimentary letters about my publications. They may have been under the influence of the same drug as I was taking. Maybe the drug experiment is extremely wide in scope. It is very likely that most of my readers know about it and consider my articles not as an objective contribution, but as a drug-induced sample of behavior. Am I like a fly caught in a glass and watched from the outside?

Now something comes to my mind which makes my heart skip a beat: Tobey, my little four-year-old friend. He was so bright and eager when we were together, but he changed into such a listless little fellow after he was transferred to the children's ward. Had he been doped? Was our love for each other chemical too?

Today I am trying to analyze the exact relation between and among people who were taking the same drug, the one I was taking at that time. It seems as if such people understood each other well when talking and joking but could not agree on the realities of living. At least this was the case with my husband and me. For example, Zuzu wanted to live in an upper-class house and neighborhood and associate exclusively with conventional, wealthy Jews; whereas I did not want such a lifestyle.

Then I search further, but something unexpected happens: the next morning when the nurse brings my medication, the white pill is missing. Instead, there is a red one.

I give it time, twenty-four hours, to ooze into my bloodstream. I receive it three times a day. Today, for the first time in many months,

I feel great anxiety, and my heart is pounding as if it wants to jump out of my skin. I keep close watch on all my thoughts and feelings and write them down in my journal as well as I can. I am relieved that the responsibility is not all mine, since my hospital chart contains a record of the drugs I have been taking and at what dosage, as well as of my behavior from day to day.

I open the door. The wild excitement of my fellow patients has vanished. They, too, must have had a change in medication. I walk through the corridor, peeking into every room to see what they are doing. Mary Anne is sewing. Anabel is watching television. Rose Marie is reading. Faith is embroidering. When I pass by, she shows me the pillow slip she is working on and asks, "Do you like it?" I answer with a vague yes and go on to Deborah's room. She is knitting.

In the afternoon I make another round. Again Mary Anne is sewing, Anabel is watching television, Rose Marie is reading, Faith is embroidering. And again she shows me her pillowcase and asks, "Do you like it?"

And Deborah is knitting.

During the week which follows, I make the rounds every morning and afternoon and always find the patients doing exactly what they did before. My mind becomes blurred, and I feel as if time stands still. My many rounds merge into one round in their uncanny sameness. But now I understand: it is the new medication which forces the patients to remain with their tasks once they have started them, like the damned creatures of Hades. And last of all, I notice that I, too, am doing the same thing from morning to night: I write and write and write.

> *After having been on the new drug for forty-eight hours, I notice a strange change in my perception. I do not see people any more, instead I see symbols of abstract ideas. Sarah is a symbol of Christian charity, and Bob a symbol of understanding. Irma is a symbol of depravity, since she is a prostitute. Also actions seem symbolic rather than real. For example . . .*

The above sentence will never be finished. Before I am able to complete it, the door opens and the nurse gives me a letter. It is addressed to me. I tear the envelope open and read:

> *As of tomorrow, you are discharged from Valley View with a diagnosis of arrested tuberculosis.*

The experiment is completed!

Suspicions

Now that I have recovered, I find myself in a new ambiguous situation. I have accepted temporary employment at St. Mary-of-the-Woods, a college operated by Roman Catholic sisters who are cloistered in an adjacent convent. My tuberculosis is completely arrested, but my physician feels that I am still too weak to return to my former position with all its pressures of teaching at a graduate school in a large university. Part-time work at St. Mary, a small undergraduate college, seems like a good transition between my complete passivity at the hospital and the heavy load which I would have to shoulder should I return to my previous position. My work will consist of being a consultant in the library, of giving German conversation lessons to the dean of the college, and of giving occasional lectures in various classes. I have moved into the layfaculty house and will start my work next week.

Here I am with the Sisters of Providence. I have not opened my diary for two weeks. I am not really in the mood to write, but I must. It is so quiet outside. I can see the lake and a statue of the Blessed Virgin through the window. I am sitting at the desk of the rare book room at St. Mary's College; I have selected this place to write because I can feel the inspiration of the people who, for many decades, have conducted their search for spiritual enlightenment in these very surroundings. The rare book room is large, wood-paneled, with a big fireplace which looks as if it has never been used. The walls are covered with ancient books suggesting parchment and dust.

Things have been so strange lately. It is as if everything and everybody knows and I don't. As if books were given to me or put where I will see them, or incidents related to me containing a message. But what is it? The bridge says something, leading over a narrow brook from the crowd of college girls with painted faces and short shirts to the convent of the sisters, where time stands still. Spanning the gap between the twentieth century and the Middle Ages, it seems to say: "Take your choice."

The Angelus rings. When I raise my eyes to follow its sound, I see a cross clear against the sky. The nuns walk silently in their black garbs. What do they know that I don't know? A park surrounds the old convent and the Renaissance church with evergreens, statues of saints, and birds—so many birds, loud and strange. They, too, seem to say something, to know the mystery of the cloisters. The warm air makes me feel drowsy. A legend comes to mind, a poem long forgotten. I walk as if in a dream.

There is another bridge: I can see it through the window. It leads over the lake into the fog—slow, silent, and inexorable. I glance back at the room. It is like the library in an old castle described on the first page of a novel. I am a figure in a novel. I have felt it for a long time, walking around like a somnambulist, as if I were acted upon by a strange force.

To my right are two paintings that depict a library cluttered with volumes. They are almost like miniatures of the larger scene of which I am a part. It, too, may be a small image of a world still larger, as the atom is an image of the solar system.

The window behind me is covered by drapes, the pattern of which is a white unicorn on green background, then another unicorn and another. The warm air creates a slight ripple in the curtain, as if a shudder would seize the herd of unicorns.

There is a toy over the fireplace: an artificial bird covered with jewels singing a soft melody in a gilded cage. When I wind it the third time, the sound becomes shrill, the bird stops, and there is silence.

In the corners are three wooden cranes with huge wings. The inscription says they were made in India. Their presence brings to mind Schiller's poem in which a flock of cranes led two murderers to confess their guilt. I also notice a black urn decorated with gold mosaic circles and a crucifix made of alabaster under a cover of glass. Cranes, an urn, a crucifix—guilt, death, and resurrection. The scene is set for a great play that is about to unfold. I am a figure in the drama.

There have been so many riddles, so many secrets here which I have tried to discover. But during the last few days, it all has begun to make sense. The hints, the books, the themes: they all speak about one thing, death. Now I know. And looking back, this may be what they have been trying to tell me: I must die.

It was the day after Palm Sunday when I suddenly understood. I thought: Gethsemane. And then I knew.

Now I must hurry. For me death does not mean the same as for the sisters in their solemn black garbs and for the college girls with their short skirts and painted faces. For me there is no hope of a hereafter. You see, I am Jewish.

It is late and I am getting weary. I have left the rare book room and have returned to my own room in the layfaculty house. The rich color of the ascetic bed. Above the desk is a print of a medieval scene with loud and piebald figures tumbling all over between the gables of strange houses. To my left, a chest; above it, Christ's picture illuminated by the glow of the lamp. On the chest: a candleholder, a bowl with red apples, *Man and His Symbols* by Carl Jung, *The Journals* by Soren Kierkegaard. It is like an altar. I am so much at peace.

Every evening I sat with some of the layfaculty in a small living room and asked many questions about Christianity. They were fascinated by my search. Once, when I first had this delightful feeling that my wheels were spinning fast, I said to a sister, half jokingly: "I think I am suffering from incipient schizophrenia." She replied: "I don't understand these fancy words." I am very different to nuns—faculty and nuns only talk to each other about college matters.

At that time—especially during the Christ delusion, which I will explain—I felt blissful, thrilled, and excited (with some short depressions between delusions).

But soon the vacant space within me caused by my long withdrawal from the world begins to fill again with strange images which ooze slowly but inexorably out of the depth of my soul. I am sure I was sent to St. Mary for a purpose which I have to discover on my own. I am convinced that I must search for the role I am meant to play in the mysterious religious drama which is unfolding around me.

Many of my insights and discoveries occur on my walks through the convent garden during the long evenings. On those walks I enter the Perpetual Adoration Chapel and hear the sisters praying—their murmuring voices hardly audible, their faces turned towards the Eternal Light. On these walks I see the novices returning to the convent at night in pairs, forming a long row of white veils which gradually merge into the white stones in the distance.

The garden is like a maze with many pathways to be discovered and explored. One night I find a little trail so well hidden between evergreens that I have not seen it before. I push the branches aside and follow the path. It turns to the left and then to the right and then it goes downhill with crude steps leading through the grass to a grotto, a cavern made of small white stones. There is a statue inside. I read the inscription on it with great effort: OUR LADY OF LOURDES. Our Lady is enveloped in darkness, but her deathly white face is still visible in the dusk—her head bent slightly forward, a melancholic smile on her lips. At her feet lighted candles are flickering in red and green glasses. Left and right of the Madonna are two large candles in glass containers. There are inscriptions on the glass: INTENTION on the left side and CONVERSION on the right side. The candle on the right is lit. Someone must be praying for my conversion!

♥

About that time, a day approaches which is of utmost importance to the sisters: Obedience Day. It is the day when each nun receives a letter from the Reverend Mother telling her what her mission for the coming year will be.

Against all reason, I have a glimpse of hope that in my mailbox, too, there might be a letter telling me what role would be assigned to me. But my box is empty. The sisters stand around in groups and talk about their assignments, but no one talks to me.

Fall is approaching. Soon the leaves will turn. The birds will fly south. The sisters will start their new missions, and the students will return to school. My work at the college will soon be completed. What will I do? I have no home, no mission. I have no husband and have resigned from my position at the university. (Before Zuzu and I separated, I stayed at Purdue Monday through Friday and then took a one-hour train ride to Zuzu in Indianapolis, staying there from Friday evening to Monday

79

morning. However, by 1961 he treated me so badly that I just didn't return to him. He would not talk to me, would go out to see an Orthodox Jewish friend and his wife leaving me at home, would say my cooking was dog food, and forced me to live on $360 a month. Once I was hospitalized he became friendly again.)

Sadly I stroll through the convent gardens, deep in thought. When I look up, I find myself in the cemetery. Rows and rows of tombstones, one exactly like the other. The graves of the Sisters of Providence. The stones bear the dead sisters' names on one side and RIP on the other side. RIP, "Rest in Peace." Will this be my mission for the future?

The first delusion which took shape within me after my move to St. Mary was the Dreyfus interpretation. At that time I believed that some of my delusions were preceded by certain cues which were meant to give me a hint regarding the specific nature of the forthcoming delusion. What follows is an example of this strange notion.

One evening I enter the living room of the layfaculty house, where most of us gather at that time to rest and to chat about the events of the day. The people living in the layfaculty house are all women but not nuns. Many of the layfaculty members live off campus. Some are Protestant. There is a rule that sensitive subjects (religion, psychology, philosophy, history) must be taught by Catholics, while nonsensitive subjects (math and the sciences) may be taught by Protestants.

On that evening I find only Elca, a black history teacher, playing checkers with a white physical-education teacher whose name I have forgotten. The latter looks very Germanic, with blond hair, blue eyes and an athletic body. Elca wears a black-and-white checkered vest, which resembles the checkerboard on which she is playing.

The first thing that strikes me is that the two women are of a different race, and the second thing is that a black-and-white checkered pattern is repeated twice, once on Elca's vest and once on the checkerboard. I start to engage in free associations to the first observation, namely to "different race," and my associations seem to center around the fact that people of different race tend to persecute each other. The associations go as follows: "Negroes, slavery, genocide, Hitler, concentration camps, etc." Then I attempt to produce associations to the black-and-white checkered designs: "Buying materials to make a dress, checkered designs make me look fat, stripes are more flattering, stars and stripes, we won

World War II, war is bad, dead soldiers, forgotten heroes, Arlington Cemetery, Memorial Day, Indianapolis Speedway, checkered flag, car races."

Then I stop, because I have found what I was looking for: one term which is represented twice in my associations to the scene, namely, the term "race." This word is most likely the message to be conveyed. But am I to understand race as a group of people belonging to the same stock, or as a competitive sport aimed at achieving the highest possible speed? I guess being the only Jew among Catholics, my set of mind induces me to focus on the first meaning of race.

Now you must remember my notion that some of my delusions are preceded by events which represent a key to the next riddle. Students, colleagues and sisters want to give me a little bit of help in my search. For example, the game of checkers which I have just described says, "Your next riddle will relate to race." And since one of the players is white and the other one black, it also suggests that the aspect of race that the riddle will relate to is racial persecution. I am fascinated by this linguistic system. Perhaps the FBI, the CIA and similar agencies communicate in this manner. What an exciting life!

The next day while my eyes peruse the shelves in the library, I see a Jewish encyclopedia consisting of many volumes. I feel certain that the day before it was not there. Have they put it here just for me? To tell me something? The backs of some of the volumes are torn to pieces. Was this done in revenge?

Then one volume catches my eye. The spine reads AARON TO DREYFUS, and the next one reads DREYFUS TO FREUD. From the moment I see the name Dreyfus, I know that I have come closer to the secret of St. Mary and to the strange circumstances which have brought me here.

The Dreyfus case! It happened more than seventy years ago. Capt. Alfred Dreyfus, the only Jew in the French Officer Corps, was falsely accused of treason. The army officers responsible for the false accusation formed a clique. They all had been educated at the famous Jesuit school in Paris. This is all I can remember. The encyclopedia tells me the rest. I turn the pages with trembling hands and suddenly come upon a name with a familiar sound: Jules Guerin, allegedly the leader of seven thousand anti-Semitic shock troops which were roaming the streets of Paris during the days of violence and civil war following the Dreyfus case. Jules

Guerin. It sounded familiar; oh, yes, the name of the founder of the Sisters of Providence was Guerin. Mother Theodore Guerin. Was she involved in the Dreyfus case?

Then the lights go out. The library is about to close. I go back to my room. Yes, I read the code correctly. The code said that the next riddle would be related to racial persecution. The Dreyfus case! In looking back over the last few days, I am convinced that I can now explain many of the strange things that happened to me. I am convinced that everybody was trying to draw my attention to the Dreyfus case for reasons that I do not know.

The name Dreyfus means "three feet" when translated from German into English. I see so many of the students walking on crutches. Perhaps they mean to tell me, "Dreyfus, three feet." For when you use a crutch, you are like a person walking on three feet: two feet of your own and one substitute foot, the crutch. I even saw one student walking on her own two legs without any trouble, until she saw me; then she started to use the crutch which she carried in her hands. Three feet—Dreyfus. That is what she wanted to tell me.

Next I remember the teachers in the faculty house. One evening when I came home they all were walking barefoot. They wanted to make me think of feet so that I would finally think of Dreyfus; they knew that *Fuss* was the German word for foot.

And then there is Sister Mary Elizabeth. I said after a conversation the content of which I have forgotten: "I am afraid I put my foot into a hornet's nest." And she replied, "It is too bad you have only two feet, because we have so many hornet's nests."

Only two feet. Did she not say this to make me think of three feet and Dreyfus? How slow I am in comprehending! But if the teachers and students want to tell me something about Dreyfus, why don't they talk to me directly? Why do they disguise their messages? I do not know.

Convinced that Mother Theodore Guerin was involved in the Dreyfus case, I go back to the pitch-dark library at night and unlock the door. With a flashlight I go from floor to floor and from bookshelf to bookshelf. I hear strange crackling noises but ignore them. Am I looking for documents on Mother Guerin? I do not know. Here I am, searching with a flashlight in a dark library tonight for a secret, the nature of which is unknown to me.

The next day I mention Dreyfus to Sister Mary Elizabeth and to Father Benedict. Father Benedict does not seem to know about the case. Sister Mary Elizabeth remembers but acts as if she fails to understand the present significance of the past events. But they do not fool me for a minute. And from speaking to Sister Mary Elizabeth, I learn something of great importance. She pronounces the name Dreyfus in a manner which is different from mine. She does not say "Dryfus," as I am used to saying. Instead, she says "Drayfus," which is a way of pronouncing the name I have never heard before. The incident in the church, which I am about to tell, will show the great significance of what I learned from Sister Mary Elizabeth.

I am sitting in my pew and listening to the Litany of the Saints. The priest says, "Holy Mary." The congregation responds, "Pray for us." Then the priest says, "Holy Mother of God." And the congregation responds, "Pray for us."

"Holy Virgin of Virgins."	"Pray for us."
"St. Michael."	"Pray for us."
"St. Gabriel."	"Pray for us."
"St. Raphael."	"Pray for us."
"All you holy angels and archangels."	"Pray for us."
"All you holy orders of blessed spirits."	"Pray for us."
"St. John, the Baptist."	"Pray for us."
"St. Joseph."	"Pray for us."

Each time the name of a saint is said by the priest, the congregation responds with "Pray for us." "Pray for us." "Pray for us." The prayer is long. It lulls me into a dreamlike state, but suddenly something strange happens. I sit up in my pew and listen to the voice behind me. The voice does not say "Pray for us." It says "Drayfus," "Drayfus," which sounds just like "Pray f' us." And then another voice says, "Drayfus." Finally the whole crowd does so: "Drayfus, Drayfus, Drayfus." I realize this is done for my benefit. Some of the sisters to my left and to my right look at me furtively to see if I finally understand.

Now I know that I am on the track of something very important, and I double my effort to penetrate the secret of the Dreyfus case.

As time goes on, I feel more and more that God sent me to St. Mary's on a mission and that it is God's will that I should detect something of great importance to the order. The founder of the order, Mother Guerin, is about to be canonized. She is about to become a saint. Perhaps it is my mission to show that she was involved in the Dreyfus case. Therefore, she can never become a saint.

It is a difficult task. Captain Dreyfus was sentenced in 1894. Mother Guerin died in 1856. The sisters must have forged the date so no one would know her crime. I search in old books and documents made of parchment, but I cannot find what I am looking for. Perhaps Jules Guerin, the leader of anti-Semitic hordes, is related to Mother Guerin. But I soon find that the name Guerin is almost as frequent in France as the name Johnson in this country.

One morning I wake up, weary from my search and knowing that I have been searching for a connection which does not exist. Then the days become gray and meaningless, and I know I have to look for new mysteries.

♥

It did not take long until I made a new discovery. I had noticed for some time that people who spoke to me tended to use certain phrases which I had used when writing this manuscript. The only incident of this kind which I can find in my diary is the following: a delivery man brings me a small safe which I bought to keep my diary in. As he puts the safe down, he says, "This is a heavy little fellow."

To my great amazement, I remember that I used the same expression, "little fellow," several times in my story about Tobey. I feel a slight suspicion. Is it possible that someone reads my diary? It is difficult to imagine, since it is always locked in a suitcase except when I work on it.

One day, before going to dinner, I wrote a note in which the following phrase was used, "Why not put two and two together?" I shall later disclose the context in which I used this phrase. Now I only wish you to know that I put the note into my purse and went to dinner.

When I sit down at the dinner table, I notice that the woman next to me has put a variety of objects on the table in front of her plate. Scanning them quickly, I notice that they are arranged in pairs: two keys, cigarettes and matches, a pencil and paper. It is obvious that there is a common element between the members of each pair. With another pair the connection is less obvious; it is a knife and a bottle of pills, which

I presume to be for one of the students, since this woman next to me is the college nurse. An idea jumps up in my mind: the pills and the knife also have something in common, namely the concept "cut"; the student for whom the pills were prescribed is sick and therefore has to cut classes. And, of course, the knife's purpose is cutting. Thus, the pills and the knife, too, form a pair. In order to indicate that I understand that all these objects come in pairs, I add another pair: two lumps of sugar. Later, when Elca drives me to the library in her blue roadster, another pair is added to my collection; a boy and a girl are standing near a tree kissing each other. I sit down at my desk in the library, and suddenly I have a new insight. I wrote the phrase, "Why not put two and two together?" on a sheet of paper. Now the important thing to remember is the fact that I put the note in my purse immediately after I had written it. Nobody could possibly have seen the note. Yet at the dinner table, the nurse had done just what I had suggested: she had put two and two together—two keys, cigarettes and matches, etc.

Vague thoughts of mental telepathy run through my mind. There are two possibilities: either the people in the dining room can read my mind and in this way knew that I had been thinking, just before dinner, of putting two and two together; or, perhaps I can read their minds, and the reason I wrote a note about putting two and two together was that they had, in fact, thought about it. Neither sounds very convincing. It must be that people can read, by some mechanical device, what I have written in seclusion.

It is just a suspicion. After all, how can one devise an invisible apparatus which makes it possible to read what someone else is writing in a closed room? But now a statement in Rebecca's letter comes to mind. I had asked Rebecca, my friend and student, to send me several pads of writing paper, the kind I was used to writing on. She replied jokingly, "What kind of paper are they using there? Are they writing on illuminated manuscripts?"

Maybe this meant that the paper I am writing on is illuminated by invisible rays so that my writing can be observed or even photographed. Maybe Rebecca's question was a roundabout way of suggesting this to me. I try to test my assumption and, in so doing, I experience an amazing correspondence between what I write and how people behave toward me.

One day I write on a piece of paper, "Eleventh Commandment: Thou shalt not snoop" (meaning, "Don't read my personal notes"). Then I put the note in my purse and go to dinner. I immediately see a long table in front of the one where I am accustomed to eating. There are students sitting at that table. This is an arrangement very different from the one I am used to. I count the number of students at the long table: there are eleven. Then everybody in the dining room begins singing: "Happy birthday to you. . . ." This is a frequent event, but usually it is followed by: "Stand up, stand up. . . ." Then the name of the birthday child is revealed, and considerable applause follows. This time the "stand up" part, the name, and the applause are omitted. I inquire of the person sitting next to me why this is the case and whose birthday we are celebrating. She answers, "I don't know. I am not snooping."

Not snooping—and eleven people sitting right in front of me! This suggests that they want to show me that my note, "Eleventh Commandment: Thou shalt not snoop," has been read.

I continue testing my belief that people are reading what I write in my room. I jokingly compose the following letter: "Dear X: The time has come to overthrow the Roman Catholic church. Please meet at 10 P.M. in my room." It is 9 P.M. I wait. A few minutes after ten, there is a knock at my door. I open it. It is one of the students. I ask her what she wants; she says she just wants to see how I am getting along. I say I am all right. She closes the door and leaves. It might be a coincidence, and yet it might not.

Right after she leaves, there follows the incident of the thunderstorm. The sky, which has been clear up to now, becomes covered with heavy clouds, and then a thunderstorm breaks loose, the likes of which I have never seen before. The lightning is so glaring, the thunder so loud, that I am convinced our house has been struck. I sit at the edge of the window, trembling and jumping each time a thunder falls. Suddenly I am struck with an idea. I run to my nightstand and write a postscript to my letter: "P.S. It was only a joke." The thunderstorm slowly subsides. It seems incredible.

Another time I wake up early on Sunday morning and see lights through the golden drapes. The lights cannot come from the sun, since my room does not face eastward. I think that it might be the lights of the machine which makes it possible to read my writings.

I write something on a piece of paper which is meant to be a joking protest against being wakened so early by these lights. I write, "Seven-thirty A.M. on Sunday: This is against union rules."

At 9 A.M. I go to church. The pews are filled with unusual people. I am told they are the students' relatives who have come for graduation. But when I look at them more closely, they do not seem like the well-to-do parents of St. Mary students. They look like rough, working-class people. Some remind me of Damon Runyan figures. The one sitting next to me looks as if, during the service, he is thinking how he can crack his next safe. I suspect they are actors, hired to impersonate members of labor unions. Again, I suspect my note has been read, even though I put it in my purse before leaving my room. I marvel at the resourceful-ness of my observers, who can populate a church with a group of actors at such short notice. It must be an enormous enterprise.

Later, during breakfast, I ask the teacher who is sitting next to me a question which I don't remember. She replies: "I don't know. My brain is not working on Sunday."

Now there is little doubt in my mind that my note complaining about being asked to work on Sunday has been read.

This notion is reinforced by a small incident which happens during the meal. The nurse, Miss O'Shenessy, says, "We always have a cold din-ner on Sunday night so that the help will not have to work."

Now my suspicion is confirmed.

This insight leads my mind to make a big jump: not only are my notes being read, but I am being observed, or photographed, during every minute of my waking and sleeping hours. Someone says: "Smile, you are on 'Candid Camera'!" Earlier someone said, "You have no privacy." What did he mean?

Another time I stand in the kitchen with a carton of milk, hesitating to use it since it belongs to someone else. Then I hear a faint voice from above: "Drink it!" It must be my imagination.

Why I am kept under observation is a problem still to be solved. Even though I am convinced that the Catholic community in which I live is doing the observing, I don't think that they have any hostile intentions. Some time ago, Sister Mary Elizabeth told me a story of a woman who, while driving a car, noticed that another car was following her. Later she found out that the man in the other car had noticed a tramp hiding in the back of her car and had followed her in order to protect her.

Perhaps she told me this story to show me that someone who is being perceived as dangerous might actually be a protector. The same thing is true for my own situation. She told me the story to show me that this is the case. The community keeps me under observation to protect me from some kind of danger, the nature of which is unknown to me.

Meanwhile, I continue to test my impression that other people can read what I write when I am alone in my room. Today I put a succession of swear words on a piece of paper and follow it with a statement something like this: "U.S. law forbids unauthorized persons to intrude into the privacy of others." There is nothing, however, in the subsequent behavior of the people who surround me which would suggest that my note has been read.

Then I write, "I am confused. Please help me. SOS." I do not get any response to this one either.

Another time I write a nonsensical note in a fictitious language: "Aragobo tugo hosearo tagolea bella ceba mick. Hu-Hu-Hu-Hu! Hem, hem." No response.

The next day I become annoyed and put down, "Take a powder! Scram! Get lost!" Again, I cannot detect any signs that my note has been read.

Later I try to test whether my observers can hear me as well as see me. When in my room, I pretend to dictate a letter. It says, "Second notice. The Honorary Scientific Society of Sigma Xi. Statement of dues, etc., etc." (This happened to be a letter which I had planned to dictate that day.) The same afternoon, Dr. Whales, one of my colleagues, tells me a long story about a friend of hers who holds a Sigma Xi key. It is amazing!

In my opinion, the observation is carried on around the clock, twenty-four hours a day. I am never alone. One afternoon I feel a sudden rush of rage about this invasion of my privacy, and immediately—without my giving it any thought—my rage turns into action. Now I am sure the observation is carried on through the large window, and that not only my writings but also my actions are being observed. I decide to block the window with furniture. I empty my drawers by putting my belongings on the floor. Then I take the drawers out of the chest and pile them on top of each other in front of the window. When the job is completed, I realize how ridiculously ineffective my work is. The pile of drawers obstructs only a small part of the window, and the rest is left open for observation.

My eyes fall on a postcard on the desk. It shows a picture by Albrecht Dürer: a pair of hands folded in prayer. I paste it on the window so it can be seen from the outside and write underneath: "Please stop watching me."

But this gentle solution doesn't satisfy me. I shall never know whether my prayer has been heard. In addition, my belligerent mood suggests a solution by which I would make it impossible for "them" to continue observing me, rather than pray for mercy.

Vacant stores, where the windows are covered with a white substance so as to prevent people from looking inside, come to mind. Then I think of children smearing windows at Halloween. I go to my bathroom. There are several jars of face creams in the medicine cabinet. I open one of them and try covering the glass with thick, white cold cream; it works. The glass ceases to be transparent. I continue feverishly. The first jar is used up, but only a small part of the window is covered; I am worried. Do I have enough cream to cover the entire window? I do not. After all my jars are empty, the upper part of the window is still clear.

My eyes fall on the cardboard prints on the wall, the works of famous masters. They are unframed pictures. I detach them, stand up on a chair, and fasten them to the top of the window. Now the entire window is covered, and no one can look in.

Today I have made a very mysterious discovery which made me forget my sadness. While ambling around in the convent garden, I absent-mindedly pick up a green leaf which has fallen from an oak tree. Walking toward the Perpetual Adoration Chapel, I finger the leaf between the thumb and forefinger of my right hand. It feels dry and solid like a piece of cloth, reminiscent of the artificial oak leaves which my mother used as decorations when serving a bowl of fruit. I try to tear the leaf, but find I can do it only with utmost effort. Then I look closely at the two torn pieces in my hand. I can hardly believe what I see. How can it possibly be that the leaf doesn't have any veins? Maybe the oak tree from which the leaf came is not an ordinary oak but some kind of rare mutation. Perhaps the whole garden is made up of rare vegetation which the sisters have acquired over the years.

Around the corner there is a pine tree. I wonder whether there is something unusual about that one, too. I look around to see whether anybody can see me and then walk through the wet grass to the tree. Standing on my toes, I try to break off a small branch covered with needles. My heart starts to pound heavily, because I am about to discover something uncanny again. My attempt to break off a small branch brings down a larger limb attached to the branch. The limb falls on my head, but is so light that it doesn't hurt me. I look up and see a hole in the tree into which the limb must have been stuck. Standing on my toes again, I have no trouble putting the limb back into the hole where it was. "What have we here?" I wonder to myself, "a collapsible tree?"

It seems that some of the vegetation, or perhaps all of the vegetation, in this beautiful garden is artificial. But why am I so excited? After all, some people do have artificial plants in their homes, so why shouldn't they have them in their gardens? No, no, I can't talk myself out of the notion that something strange is going on here. But it is getting dark, and I must postpone my investigation until tomorrow.

Today I get up early in the morning, skip breakfast and hurry back to the convent garden. The air is fresh and cool. The vegetation—real or artificial—is covered with dew, and I am eager to continue my investigation. Soon I find myself at my favorite place, a circle with a diameter of about ten feet with no vegetation. The ground is covered with pebbles. A little bench stands at the periphery, and a statue of St. Francis of Assisi decorates the middle of the circle. I sit down on the bench facing St. Francis and our eyes meet.

"What is the secret of this place, St. Francis? Why are you, who loves nature so much, surrounded by artificial plants? Are the birds and the butterflies artificial, too?" But St. Francis remains silent.

I rise from my seat, step toward the saint and put my hands on his shoulders. The statue is smaller than I am, but the pedestal underneath it brings our shoulders to the same level. St. Francis's shoulders feel strange. Not like stone, wood, or metal—or whatever statues are made of. They feel more like cardboard. Again this uncanny feeling that things are not what they seem to be, that I don't understand what's going on around me.

My watch shows that it is almost 9 A.M., and I have to hurry to Sister Elizabeth Ann's office to be on time for the German conversation lesson

90

with the sister and Father Benedict. In the afternoon, I must prepare a lecture on Thomas Mann's *Death in Venice* to be delivered in Sister Magdalene's class in comparative literature. Not much time for playing detective!

The Passion Play

I have not opened my diary for six days. During this time I have tested my notion that the convent garden is artificial. I have examined almost every tree, every bush and every statue to see whether it is real or fake. Roughly 75 percent of the garden is fake.

I am approaching a building with thick pillars in front, much like the antebellum houses in the south of the United States. The pillars look suspicious. I knock at one of them as one would knock at a door. The knock makes a hollow sound. Are the buildings unreal, too?

I am much too anxious to describe further details of my investigation. It suffices to say that at least 50 percent of the buildings within the convent are made of cardboard. My interest in further investigation of the convent has diminished.

Now my big question is, Why? What does it all mean?

I go downtown and find that the scene seems to have radically changed. An unusually large number of disabled people walk around on Main Street. Cripples are limping on their crutches in front of the hotel where I used to eat. A man whose limbs shake with palsy is standing in front of the drugstore, and another one is carrying dishes in the coffee shop. On my way from the hotel to the post office I meet two blind people with white canes. Or are they pretending?

Today the jigsaw puzzle finally falls into place. Perhaps the convent is a set in the same sense as, for example, a western town in a Hollywood studio. But is someone planning to shoot a motion picture at St. Mary? Or to perform an outdoor play? What could be the plot of this drama?

Then the solution hits me like lightning: a flash in my brain retrieves the name Oberammergau[1] from my memory bank, and now I can explain everything! The cripples, the blind, the men with palsy whom I saw are the kind of people whom Jesus healed. The sisters must be planning a passion play or a film, and somehow they are trying to connect the life of Christ with their convent, since its garden and its buildings will be part of the film. How they are going to do this is beyond me, but—after all—that's their headache. I rush downtown hoping to find a leper, but my search is in vain.

New riddles, new riddles! Why did Sister Emmanuel, whom I hardly know, stop me in the hall to say, "You stepped out of the grave"?

"What do you mean?"

"When you had tuberculosis, you were almost dead, and then you recovered miraculously." Then she gave a meaningful smile as if she had something up her sleeve. Likewise, why did my student, Rebecca, say on one of her visits: "When you became sick I felt as if it were Good Friday. But now that you are well, I feel as if it were Easter Sunday."

Sitting by the living room window of the faculty house I see Elca, one of my favorite teachers, coming up the driveway in her red Volkswagen. She must have been out on a shopping spree, because her car is filled with packages. I run out and help her carry some of the stuff into her room.

"What did you buy?"

"Oh, a skirt, two blouses and two pairs of shoes," she replies casually. "And then," she says in a mysterious tone, "I bought something for you."

"For me? What?"

"A cross," Elca whispers.

"To wear on a necklace?" I am wondering how I can tell her tactfully that such adornment is not accepted among Jews.

But she interrupts my hesitation by declaring, "Oh no, not for a necklace. It is a big cross, but not too heavy, not heavy at all."

---

[1]Oberammergau is a town in Germany, famous for the passion play performed by the inhabitants every ten years.

"May I see it?"

"It is much too big for my little Volkswagen, but you can see it tomorrow when they'll deliver it."

Statements of this kind, of which I remember very many, give me the impression that people spoke to me as if I were Jesus. But I know I am not Jesus. How can I solve this contradiction? Could it be—could it be—that everybody is trying to tell me by hints and allusions that I have been selected to play the role of Jesus Christ in the forthcoming passion play? What nonsense! I am a woman, Christ was a man; I am old (fifty-five), Christ was young; I am Jewish, Christ was Christian—no, no, what am I saying? He was a Jew, of course!

One day I read a German poem, one of my childhood favorites, to Father Benedict. It was made into a Christmas song which I was fond of singing. It begins: "Es ist ein Reis entsprungen aus einer Wurzel zart . . ." (A twig has sprung from a tender root). And after dwelling on Jesus' birth, the poem turns to the Blessed Virgin. "I don't like this part as much as I used to," I say, referring to the stanza on St. Mary. Father Benedict replies, "Familiarity breeds contempt." Familiarity? Is he referring to the Holy Virgin being my fictitious mother? Then I remember the day when Father Benedict commented on the severity of my tuberculosis: "You sacrificed yourself for your work." Again, he spoke to me as if I were Jesus!

The fact that my life—which of late has been amorphous, haphazard and meaningless—has suddenly changed to a puzzle to be solved fills me with the kind of excitement which readers of detective novels might experience when they are presented with clue after clue and with the knowledge that all seemingly meaningless details will fall into place to form one pattern revealing the solution and the meaning of the entire story.

Today, I start to have new flashes of insight. Soon these insights occur to me with such speed that I can hardly keep track of them. It is as if a beautiful blossom is opening in front of my eyes. And at the end of this period of puzzle solving, of trying to make a whole of all the strange and unusual things that have happened to me, everything falls into place, and I finally become certain that my amazing solution was correct, a solution of such grandeur, beauty, and sacredness that I can hardly believe it.

Yes, I was right! The campus of St. Mary is preparing to perform a passion play, and I am to play the role of Jesus Christ.

According to my journal, this insight occurred on May 10, 1965.

I feel sure that everyone knows about the passion play and the role I am to play in it, but for some reason, I cannot be told directly what is about to happen. Instead, I am expected to interpret the hints which I receive regarding my role, and, putting two and two together, to eventually discover the truth on my own.

Now that I know St. Mary is planning to film a passion play, I am asking myself another uncanny question: Are the sisters real nuns, or are they actresses in disguise? However, I do not ask the nuns directly.

At other times, people who seem to be teachers show wisdom far superior to what I expect. For example, some of the teachers use philosophical terms and long, high-brow sentences when they speak to me, and I do not understand what they have said. Am I surrounded by the greatest experts in philosophy and theology to help plan the great drama? My thoughts swell like a flowing river, and I begin to see St. Mary and the town as a huge camp of actors, showing their performances and hoping to be engaged. It feels like a children's fairy tale, where everything becomes possible and where every fantasy can become a reality.

My thoughts are racing, and I find it hard to concentrate. I am not sure whether I will be able to carry out the tremendous enterprise which lies ahead of me. But, paradoxically, the role of Christ is such that it can be played better by those who do not feel up to it: it is a role which demands humility and surrender.

Perhaps the great event during which I will be officially established in my role as Christ will take place on Ascension Day, the day when Christ ascended to Heaven. In anticipation of this day, I am elated and have a feeling of grandeur. I leave little notes wherever I go, appointing people to be my apostles or adding commandments to the ten revealed to Moses. Again I feel like Alice in Wonderland, surrounded by a world where every fantasy can become reality.

During the few days which are left before Ascension Day, I receive more messages than ever before. The following are some of them. I find a significant little object on the kitchen table. It is a small cap which must have been used to cover a bottle. On it the phrase "Orange Juice" is printed, but it is printed in an unusual way. One-half of the little cap is green, and the other is white. One part of the inscription is printed on the green side, namely ORA JUICE; the rest is printed on the white side. It looks something like this:

I do not remember what was written on the right bottom part of the circle.

I know that the cap was made especially to convey a message to me. I read only the part on the green side, which says ORA JUICE. I immediately translate: "ora Juice"—"ora Jews" (*ora* is the Latin word for *pray*), meaning "pray for the Jews." They want me to pray for the Jews when I go to Heaven in only a few days. It is a good joke. I am amused by their request and put a check mark next to the inscription, indicating that I have read it and that I will act accordingly. Then my glance falls upon a box of soap flakes on which the brand name ALL is printed. I put a check mark next to the "All" and then place the bottle cap on the box. My message is meant to say: "I shall pray for the Jews, but not only for the Jews; instead, I shall pray for all." Again my heart is flooded with a warm feeling of sisterhood and brotherhood.

I laugh when one day before Ascension Day I find a note by the telephone saying, "Leave messages *here.*" It takes me a few seconds to realize what is meant. I should leave the telephone messages here on earth instead of taking them with me to Heaven. I must stress that I have never thought I will really go to Heaven. Instead, I have been thinking in terms of make-believe rather than in terms of reality. But the line of demarcation becomes dimmer and dimmer.

It is 11:30 on the night before Ascension Day—another half hour until midnight. During this half hour I feel I have to get everything ready without quite knowing what and why. But I must stress again that I am thinking in terms of make-believe rather than in terms of reality. Above all, I have to reassure all my friends that I will pray for them. At 11:55 P.M. I am overcome by an irresistible urge to go out into the dark hall and put a check mark after everyone's name-sign on their doors, meaning that I will pray for them. I finish the first floor hastily and then rush off to the second floor. After my errand is completed, I fall into my bed exhausted and sleep soundly.

I am somewhat shy the next morning. It is the twenty-seventh day of May in the year 1965. Ascension Day. I stay away from people and from the outdoors. Perhaps this is the day when "they" will finally tell me about the great enterprise in which I am to play such an important part. In the late afternoon, I am unable to stand the inactivity and the loneliness of waiting any longer. Soon it will be dark. I walk slowly to the convent garden on the narrow pathways surrounded by evergreens. I look at one statue and then at another. But the statues are mute. Then I see that the church is lighted. Perhaps the sisters are assembled there, waiting for me to come in so they can tell me the great secret. But when I enter the church, the sisters are gone. I am alone.

On my way back to the house I am overcome by a spell of dizziness. I think, "And it came to pass, while he blessed them, he was parted from them, and carried up into heaven" (Luke 24:51). Two students come by and notice my unsteady gait. They hold me, one on each side, while I am walking back to my room. The spell of dizziness, I am sure, is caused by sedatives which the sisters have put into my food. They have done it for my own good, since my tension is getting unbearable.

The next morning I awake early. Ascension Day has gone by like any other day. Nothing has happened, and everything is unchanged. I feel depressed.

Perhaps I should put an end to all this guessing and spying, perhaps I should approach someone who is a leading figure in the college or convent community and tell him or her directly about my discovery regarding the passion play and my role in it. But there is always the possibility that I am mistaken and then people will think I am crazy. In addition, I enjoy the uncertainty so much that I yearn to prolong it, even though the joy is mixed with suffering. And suppose the passion play is merely a delusion, what then? It would be bad enough to be viewed as crazy, but there is something else that would be infinitely worse: the whole meaning of my life and all my expectations for the future are based on the play and my role in it. If both were figments of my imagination, what would I do? Again, as on Obedience Day, I would have to ask myself, What is *my* mission? Will the rest of my life be merely a waiting for death?

No, it would be much too risky to tell anybody what I am thinking. But then I feel a flash of light in my brain and there is an idea! Now I know what I am going to do. Instead of telling them about my discovery, I will suggest that they perform a passion play. The college has an excellent drama department and, in view of their strong emphasis on the New Testament, performing a passion play seems like a very realistic idea. Maybe it would be better at first not to mention my own role in the play.

Then another flash, and now I know how I will carry out my plan. I write on a large piece of paper:

> *There is no book like the Bible.*
> *There is no business like show business.*
> *Why not put two and two together?*

Then I put this message on the bulletin boards at the layfaculty house and at the convent. These boards are checked by faculty and staff several times daily for messages. The next day I find that my notes have been removed from both boards. Nobody makes any comment regarding my message.

♥

At the same time, strange little overtones, which bring about a new and unexpected development, are added to my insights. I believe it started on Sunday in church before the service. The lights had not been turned on yet, and it was dark. Then, suddenly, one limelight was turned on and directed upon a picture over the altar. I had been told before that it was a picture of the Apostle Peter. The picture showed him writing on a tablet which he was holding in his hand.

Why is the light directed upon Peter? Is it done to tell me something I should know? It is hard to guess what it might be. Perhaps it is relevant that Peter is writing, as I do. Or, perhaps I am not to play the role of Jesus, but instead have been selected to play the role of Peter. I am seized by deep disappointment.

But it does not last long. The incident gives my thoughts a new direction. Peter is a slang word for penis. Is the incident in the church meant to draw my attention toward the fact that I will be playing the role of a man? I am deeply shocked. My indignation is twofold. Firstly, I do not think that sexual matters should be associated with the life of Jesus. That

Jesus was a male was part of the husk and not of the kernel of his existence. And secondly, it is blasphemous, in my opinion, to use the church for any kind of sexual insinuation.

The allusions to my fictitious manhood become more frequent. The women who surround me are much friendlier than they used to be. They even wash my dishes. When the students leave the dining room and pass by me, they wiggle their hips while walking. It is amazing how everything supports my hunches about the passion play.

My relation to the village people has changed. Previously I have tended to keep the curtains of my room tightly closed because the various interpretations of my environment which I held in the past left me in doubt whether the inhabitants of the little houses facing my windows were friends or foes. But now I know that I am to play the role of Jesus and that everybody but me has known about this for a long time. Since the villagers are all Christians, I have nothing to fear. This is a Christian country, and I have been chosen for the role of Christ. Everybody is with me and for me. I am flooded by a warm feeling of sisterhood and brotherhood.

I open the drapes and sit down on the window sill in my dark room watching the lighted windows of the villagers across the lawn. And then it happens. Someone must have discovered that I am looking out of the window, and soon I am to watch the most beautiful spectacle on earth. It is meant to celebrate those who created the great passion play. The dark lawn is suddenly illuminated, most probably by limelights hidden in the grass. Mist floats in front of my window to give the scene an appearance of unearthly beauty. Then a whole regiment of fireflies is released and floats on the air above the lawn. Then come butterflies and birds. And the little lights in the village are twinkling as if to say, "We know."

I return to my room in the late afternoon. As soon as I open the door, I gasp at the scene which presents itself to me. Golden light is floating through the closed drapes. I know that the producers of the passion play have arranged this, but the beauty of the color is so overwhelming that

I perceive the light as sent by God and the producers as only instruments of divine power. I am in ecstasy.

I want to go to bed to let the light bathe my body like the caresses of a lover. Without taking off my clothes, I lie on my bed with my hands folded over my breasts. As the warm air rises and creates a wrinkle in the drapes, I open my arms in an embrace of something holy that I cannot see. I plead: "More, give me more." My nipples grow and tingle, my blood rushes into the little world between my thighs making it hot and moist, and finally a fierce tremor of my loins shakes my entire body. The lights become dimmer and dimmer. Soon I am enveloped in darkness and in blissful peace, knowing that I was as close to God as a woman can ever be.

Two days before I am scheduled to leave St. Mary, my tension becomes so great that I cannot stand it any longer. I fear that I will become insane if I continue guessing. Within the remaining two days, I will have to approach the right person, tell him or her about my suspicions, and get all the available information regarding the passion play and my role in it. I cannot bear the uncertainty any longer.

Exhausted, I sit down on my bed. In about forty-eight hours I will have to leave St. Mary. I do not know where I will go. Something has to be done immediately or I will lose my mind.

Finally I telephone Father Benedict and ask him to come and see me. When he arrives, I tell him that I am convinced that St. Mary is neither a college nor a convent. Instead it is a camp of actors, producers and stage managers getting ready to perform a passion play in which I am to play the role of Jesus Christ. The priest looks at me gravely. Then he asks me for the name and address of my nearest relative.

When, in the mental hospital, the Thorazine trickles into my bloodstream—drop by drop, day after day—slowly and almost imperceptibly my images vanish. There is no passion play, no role of Christ. It was so beautiful. Why did they have to kill my passion and bring me back into their sleepy world of bland and shallow usualness?

Now St. Mary is just a college, not a stage, and my friends are neither actors nor are they wizards. The light which caressed my body through the drapes was the light of the setting sun. Soon I begin to realize that my behavior must have seemed very strange to others.

The Thorazine trickles into my bloodstream, drop by drop, day after day, and the patterns dissolve slowly and almost imperceptibly. The drama that I experienced was within me, a drama of which the outside world knew nothing.

But sometimes at dusk, when the shadows lengthen and the earth becomes silent, my thoughts return to the days when the world was transfigured and when I planned the great passion play.

As the Thorazine closes the door to the depth of my being, the world no longer seems to have one meaning or to be governed by one cause. There seem to be many causes and much chance. Many happenings seem to be without meaning altogether. A stone rolls down a hill, a child is born, an old man dies, and there is not much reason to account for it. There are no great truths to be discovered on this earth.

"Life is like a tale told by an idiot . . . signifying nothing."

The Road to Reality

Now I want to tell you more about the mental hospital.

During the first week or so, my stay at Pineville was reasonably pleasant. I did not believe that I was in a mental hospital. I thought, in line with my spiritual delusion, that I was in a camp of actors.

There are about twenty women in the locked ward where I am hospitalized—or imprisoned. Most of them are young adults with drug problems.

The main windows of the dayroom are barred. The walls are tiled, like in a bathroom. I find this rather unpleasant. Fairly comfortable chairs and sofas, upholstered and covered with green vinyl, are grouped all over the room. There are no tables, and you have to ask for a card table if you need one.

We patients are frequently taken to several places for singing, arts and crafts, bowling, folk dancing, between-meal snacks, etc. We are also taken outdoors from time to time. There the young patients play basketball while the old ones watch, suffering from the heat and from sitting on hard wooden picnic benches.

All the planned activities are called therapies; whatever we do, the term therapy is attached to it: music therapy, art therapy, sport therapy, bibliotherapy. Perhaps snack therapy?

Bibliotherapy reminds me that I haven't told you about the little library to which we are taken every Monday. There we may check out books to keep us occupied during the week. There are no religious books available; they are strictly taboo.

Actually the patients don't read much. Most of them play games like checkers, aggravation, poker and the like. When they come back from meals, they run to the card tables. Within seconds they are engrossed in their games. Pauses are dangerous, they make you think.

We are always in a group, never alone. No patient is supposed to ever be by herself. For example, when you go to the john, an aide goes with you and stands outside till you are finished.

We are not even permitted to carry purses or wear clothes with pockets. Possessions which we might need such as combs, brushes, or lipsticks are put in niches that look like mailboxes in hotels; the so-called mail board is located behind the nurses' counter, and you can ask for your stuff whenever you want. I find this rather convenient because we can think of other things, especially about the forthcoming passion play, instead of dipping into our purses all the time with the nerve-racking question, Where did I put my damn comb?

But I have one real problem; I'm suffering from a chronically dripping nose and require one or two pocket-size packages of Kleenex a day. Question: If I can't have a purse or pocket, where shall I put my Kleenex and where shall I dispose of it? Dream Reader, if you are a woman you know the answer already: in my bra, of course.

Thus, before we are taken to breakfast, I ask for my box of Kleenex, take out a big handful, and put it in my bra. The nurse whispers to the aide: "Stuffs it all into her bosom." Then she gets my chart and writes it in there for the psychiatrists to see! And intimidated little Edith, instead of saying: "Where—oh where—am I supposed to put my Kleenex?" just ambles off letting whoever reads my chart believe that I have a mammilary-hoarding complex, or something of this kind.

There are further problems connected with my dripping nose; during the day I discover that if I stuff the used Kleenex back into the bra, pretty soon I get into trouble trying to distinguish between the clean and the dirty ones. So the next day I put all my Kleenex into the left cup, intending to use the right cup as a trash can. Thank God, I look in the mirror before anyone can see me. Oh boy, what a sight! One gigantic breast and one that looks almost flat in comparison. And the staff being on the lookout for hidden jackknives or little revolvers! So I even out my cargo and add my problem to the long list of other problems of life which I have never solved.

♥

Frankly, the hospital is a relief after the last days at St. Mary. I feel I have acquired a role in life, that I have a niche. I am a mad person in a place intended for mad people, or perhaps an actress among actors? When I arise in the morning, the radio plays cheerful music that makes me feel like dancing.

Especially on Mondays and Thursdays I feel good. These are the days when we go downstairs to occupational therapy for one hour. When I went there for the first time, I walked around and looked at all the thousand things that I could do: carving wood, designing patterns for curtains or tablecloths, or hammering on shining metal. Everything was bright and colorful, much like the lab of a magician.

The OT (Occupational Therapy) teacher, Mrs. Fender, asks me if I have decided what to do, and I inquire, "May I paint in oil?" And she replies, "Sure thing, you may!"

Soon I am seated on a stool with canvas, palette, and brush. I see a little cloth doll that looks like *Zäpfelkern* (Pinocchio) and seat it right in front of me for inspiration. I paint a little house, a tree, a fence, a lawn, a path, the sky and clouds. The finished product looks like a cross between a third-grade drawing and a Grandma Moses. It is miraculous for me that I can think of trees, let the thought trickle from my brain into my hand and, whoops, the trees are on the paper. This is my first attempt at painting in oil. High up in the sky I paint a tiny little bird with open beak that sings, "coo-coo, coo-coo!"

I ask the doctor if I can change my schedule, go to OT more often, and he says, "No." But the doctor does not yet control my thoughts, and I spend much time on the ward creating my next picture of fantasy. It will be a design with horizontal rows covering the whole canvas. Each row will consist of a bright green pine tree followed by a big red mushroom covered with white polka dots. Then another tree, another mushroom, until the whole canvas is covered. Now I have something to look forward to every day, namely my next OT session. When the picture is finished, it will recreate the spirit of Grimms fairy tales, which nourished me when I was a child.

The day that I have feared for a long time has come. Today I must appear before the staff of our hospital to be evaluated and diagnosed. The nurse tells me that I shall be asked questions and admonishes me to answer them with honesty and precision.

The one thing I worry about most is my looks. I have peeked in the mirror many times a day this week, but I always stay about a yard away, and from a distance I look good. But it is hard to be deceived. I haven't fixed my hair for umpteen weeks and wear, day after day, the same white nylon blouse with big blue flowers and a bow. I am less worried about the questions I will be asked than about my appearance.

The conference room is closed to the dayroom where I spend most of my time, together with the other ladies (that's what they call us) on my ward. Today I try to sit real close to the short hallway leading to the conference room, and —thank God—the aide does not give me her usual, "Miz Joelson, don't sit by yourself, go over there, play checkers with the other ladies." I guess she understands.

While waiting I develop a new symptom. I have to run to the toilet every few minutes to arrange my hair, with my hand trembling lest I be called while out of the room.

And now I am sitting at the head of a long table with people, mostly men in white coats, left and right all the way down the table. I recognize psychiatrists and nurses, all looking straight at me. I can't peruse my jury, or my audience (depending on how you view the situation) because Dr. Dalton, the young psychiatrist who is supposed to demonstrate my case, immediately begins to question me.

I did not enter this event into my diary until much later. Thus, I do not remember the most fascinating questions. I am also ashamed to tell you that I found some questions fascinating. I believe that the patient is not supposed to be fascinated by the questions, however fascinated the psychiatrist may be by the answers.

The first question: "Do you still believe that you are living on a stage?"

As I write these pages, I feel my heart pounding: I am thinking that you, Dream Reader, will see me humiliated and degraded.

I reply with hesitation: "No, most things are real now. But . . ."

"But what?"

"But sometimes when I am all alone, I look out of the window at the sky, the trees, the flowers, and I get a feeling of enchantment, a fairy-tale feeling right in the middle of the hospital."

Silence, interrupted by a young man with a white coat and a crew cut sitting far away at the other end of the table. "Could you repeat what you just said?"

I feel my face becoming pale and my intestines going into a spasm. Is this a test of sanity? Then I stammer: "When I look out of the window of my room, it looks as if it were a fairy tale."

The crew-cut doctor shakes his head. We do not seem to understand each other.

I listen with utmost effort as an older man bends forward to ask another question: "Did you really believe that you are going to play the role of Christ in films or dramas?"

"Oh, yes."

The man turns to his colleagues, "Can I borrow the patient's chart just for a minute?" A nurse hands him a manuscript-like thing between two metal covers. My questioner gets lost in red tape.

"Let's see, now. You are Joelson, Edith. Occupation: Professor. How can you be a professor when your head is all confused?"

"My head was fine before this happened."

"Well, if you say so. I see you are from Vienna. A lovely town. When did you come to the United States?"

"In nineteen hundred and thirty-nine."

"Why did you come? Was it the war?"

"I was a refugee from Hitler."

"But are you Jewish?"

"Yes, I am."

"But what is all that hoopla about Christ if you are Jewish?"

"I am Jewish by descent and ancestry and also by my solidarity with the victims of the holocaust. But I have never observed the Jewish faith."

"Why not?"

"Because my family did not observe it."

"Well, what religion did you then observe? Did you observe Christianity?"

"No, we did not hold any religious faith. We celebrated Christmas every year, but not as a religious holiday."

"Being Jewish, not going to the synagogue, celebrating Christmas— perhaps the entire family is borderline psychotic."

"No, Doctor. There were multitudes of Jews in Austria and Germany who were assimilated to other Austrians or Germans and who knew very little about Judaism. They were not psychotic, they were just different from other Jews."

"But why do you want to play the role of Christ?"

"I thought it would be wonderful to do so."

By that time *my* Dr. Dalton resumed his demonstration: "Do you still believe in the passion play and in your role as Christ?"

106

"No, I believe it less and less. But now I suspect that my role of Christ is a metaphor. A passion play is a symbolic story of my life and of every human life."

Now Dr. Dalton raises his voice: "This is not true. It makes no sense. Forget these fantasies."

But I say strongly and with conviction: "They may seem fantasies to scientists and doctors, but at St. Mary's they are believed by everyone."

Then Dr. Dalton almost screams: "No one believes your fantasies. That you believe them shows that you are SICK!"

And thus the exorcism of a Jewish woman possessed by Jesus Christ comes to an end.

Then a new voice comes towards me, the voice of an intern or a resident physician. Looks like a student: young, bearded, and with ash-blond hair that almost reaches to his shoulders. He has not said a word during my trial, but now he rises and speaks: "Dr. Joelson believes that her delusions about the passion play are symbolic, like metaphors. This is a big step toward mental health. If someone says she hears the real voice of God, she is psychotic; but if a preacher says, 'Listen to the voice of God,' he is normal because his pronouncement is a metaphor."

I put my head upon the table and sob. Someone understands me.

Dr. Dalton asks Mazie, the aide, to take me back immediately to my ward. We walk through the short hallway, open the door to the dayroom, and find, lo and behold, that it is empty: not a soul—no patients, no attendants, and no nurses.

Mazie looks at the empty room and seems out of kilter. "I am supposed to be on ward three and I can't leave you here alone," she whines. I comfort her, with evil thoughts in mind, as you will see, Dream Reader. "Oh, I'll be all right—I feel much better."

But Mazie doesn't hear me because she is hollering excitedly into the phone. "Why doesn't anybody tell me y'all are going on a field trip? What am I supposed to do now with my patient? Can you find someone to come up here? But make it fast, I gotta go to three this minute."

She turns to me: "I'll have to run now, Honey. You be good, and there will be someone with you in a jiffy." Then she vanishes.

I crack the door to the conference room noiselessly and sit down on a chair behind the door, protected from their sight by a merciful turn of the hallway. I close my eyes and pretend to sleep.

I can't hear every word, but bits of conversation reach me. They seem to be discussing my own case! I hear mostly the voice of Dr. Dalton. Then I recall he is being supervised by an older physician regarding the way he handles me and other patients. I suspect my trial is both his and mine.

A female voice asks something like, ". . . only Christ . . . other delusions?"

A deep, male voice: "Tell us about the others."

Then Dr. Dalton: ". . . she thought the other TB patients . . . to get some money out of her."

The deep voice again: ". . . causes of this delusion . . . ."

Dalton's reply is long, but all I hear is "guilt complex." Then some drilling starts on the street, and I find myself excluded from my trial.

But my fantasy takes over, and I put myself on the defendant seat and speak to my fictitious jury. And what I say silently in my mind is a confession:

At age eleven I was too weak to go to school. I had contracted pleurisy the year before which left me vulnerable to infections. The doctor said I should be taught at home. Thus we engaged a teacher named Eudora.

Eudora had a face of tender beauty, more like an angel than a real person. Her face was slim and regular, her skin all white and pink, her hair dark blond, her eyes light blue. But this perfect head grew on an almost crippled body, a body that was short and thin, barely supported by a badly curved spine. I think she was a hunchback, but I never used this word in speech or thought.

She was extremely smart and educated, and taught me well till I returned to school when I was twelve.

It's hard to say how old she was, since children cannot judge the age of grown-ups. The only description that I can think of is late youth.

She lived with us the year she taught me and stayed long after that—for many years—as a guest, or paying guest, and friend of the whole family. She was all mind and brain and never talked to me about men, or dates, or marriage. She had a sister named Naomi who was less smart but otherwise much like Eudora. I did not know the sister very well.

Eudora and Naomi were Sephardic Jews, which means their ancestors had lived in Spain or Portugal. Eudora made a living by teaching subjects that were not taught in public schools, like art, religion,

108

foreign literature. Naomi taught piano, I believe. They barely survived in a country as poor as Austria.

After the year 1935, I lost contact with the two sisters. In 1939 my whole family came to America.

And now I am approaching the point that burns.

Dream Reader, I have long forgotten that I was, in fantasy, talking to the staff meeting of the mental hospital. The drill out on the street still fills my ears, and I can't hear what's going on. I suspect the meeting has adjourned and the aide who was supposed to replace Mazie never came. So let me continue to tell you, Dream Reader, what I was thinking on that day:

When my family came to the United States, we were not quite penniless as many other refugees. We owned $5,000 dollars. I do not know where this $5,000 came from, but I believe we had transferred this sum from Austria to a foreign bank some years ago. Legally the money belonged to my mother, but it was a gentlemen's agreement that my jobless brothers and I could use a part of it until we had found a job. We further agreed that after that we would support our mother with our earnings, and the remaining money would stay untouched in order to give her the assurance that she wouldn't be penniless if we would lose our jobs.

We were informed—I don't remember how—that Eudora and Naomi were still in Vienna and that they could not come to the United States because they did not have the money to pay the fare. I do not remember whether we did send the money and it was too late or whether we decided not to send the money. Be that as it may, Eudora and Naomi never came, and no one has ever heard from them.

Even though the money belonged to my mother, I could have appealed to her conscience. But I did not.

And need we worry about Naomi and Eudora? Is it fair for a Jewish refugee family to own $5,000, to own any spare money at all, while the cadavers are burning in the concentration camps? Dr. Dalton, is there a guilt complex or is it guilt?

109

Thorazine

During this first period at the hospital I was full of mischievous humor and eager to engage in pranks.

Today I feel a peak of this rebellion. It is July the Fourth, Independence Day, and here I am in shackles.

I want to go to the Catholic services today; it's Sunday. The hospital supplies Protestant and Roman Catholic services; however, you are permitted to go to the Protestant services only if you are a Protestant and to the Catholic services only if you are a Catholic. If you are a Jew, you can have a Rabbi come to see you if you wish.

Dream Reader, I would like you to know that it is a matter of indifference to me whether I go to Protestant, Catholic or Jewish services or to no services at all. But I want to play the freedom game, to try out my wings, to make high waves. This country is based on the principle of religious freedom, and today, on July the Fourth, I am forcefully kept out of the Catholic services. As the ladies of my ward are led through the halls like a flock of geese, we pass the door to the auditorium where the Catholic mass is about to begin. Suddenly I scream at the top of my voice, "Father, Father!" In my fantasy I see the priest hurling himself out of the door, grabbing me and thundering, "Let this child attend the service of her choice."

Instead two huge, muscular, heavyweight boxing champions wearing white coats, who are called attendants, rush towards me. They grab my whole body with their mere four hands with such might that I feel enclosed, as if in an iron cage.

110

I am five feet, three and one-half inches; my weight is 117 pounds; and my bone structure is small. My age is fifty-five. Yet the fear of a woman who imagines things is so powerful that those in charge begin to imagine things, too: they view me as powerful and dangerous. A few minutes later, my husband receives a call from Dr. Dalton, who says that I am violent and dangerous and will have to receive shock treatments.

As I learn later, Zuzu refuses to sign a permission slip. He will be right over and talk to me. He says he's known me for more than twenty years; I do not have a violent bone in my body. I like pranks and rebellion, but I am in full control and can conform if I can be convinced that it is temporarily necessary.

Should I receive a sizeable number of shock treatments, he argues, I might not be able to say smart things to students, which I will have to do until the age of sixty-seven, when I retire.

Instead of shock treatments, I receive Thorazine. No one told me in advance that this was going to happen. My name was merely added to a long list of names which the medication nurse calls out from the counter three times a day.

"Miz Abbott, Miz Chancer, Miz Endicott" . . . and then, unexpectedly, "Miz Joelson," which means I have to join the line, wait for my turn, and then swallow something which will cure me of paranoid schizophrenia.

If I had diabetes or cancer, I'd swallow anything that might cure me, but this disease that you are going to play the role of Christ is a tricky sort of disease. It is blissful, and I hate to give it up.

While waiting in line, I wonder if the medicine will be a liquid, a tablet, or a capsule. If it is a capsule, it is a cinch to hide it in my mouth and later spit it out. I know that people who want to commit suicide in a hospital collect sleeping pills that way. But I don't want to commit suicide; hell no, my life is much too thrilling to do that. Just imagine all the things that went on in my head in just a short span of time: I met the poor people in the TB hospital, I participated in an experiment on psychedelic drugs, and I am—who knows—going to play the role of Christ. I learned secret codes and lived in a plastic convent. I met the sweetest, tiniest, most delicate, most curious, most adventurous and most mischievous little boy, and we loved each other! Anyway, I want to spit the pill into the toilet.

111

Two more ahead of me and then it is my turn. I will not let them cure me. I will not return to the bland and trivial world of normal people. The line gets shorter, and I see it is a liquid. I take the little plastic cup and put the small amount of yellowish liquid into my mouth. I then put my hands around my neck, go into contortions of nausea and spit so that it looks like puking. (I learned this as a child when I had to take cod liver oil.) I figure that when they see my delicate stomach cannot take the smell and taste of Thorazine they will give me capsules, right?

Wrong. The two boxers who did not like my Catholic devotion appear again in a split second and hold me down while the nurse gives me the medication by injection.

I have five hours until the next installment of Thorazine will be due. This gives me time to practice holding a liquid in my mouth without swallowing it and looking natural while doing so. It's real easy as long as you don't speak, but suppose someone asks you a question?

Try it, Dream Reader. Try to fill your mouth with water and say "Testing, one, two, three, testing" and see what happens. Thus, I have to drink my potion after each meal and at bedtime.

Thorazine and similar drugs have been praised because they have emptied mental hospitals and permitted "those less fortunate ones" to resume their proper place in the community. My foot!

Let me tell you how this medicine affects *me*. I become drowsy, indifferent and depressed. I welcome it at bedtime because it makes me sleep so well, but who wants to sleep during the day, especially in the middle of a revolution?

I notice the change most drastically when we (the ward ladies) go down to OT. My coordination has become very bad, and even getting there is quite fatiguing. I look around the workshop. Is this the place that I viewed as a magician's lab only a short time ago? Now I see a sad-looking assembly of wool, wood, paint and cloth with dismal-looking people slowly stitching and carving like robots or slaves.

The teacher says, "You have finished two oil paintings, do you want to do another one?"

"No, I would not know what to paint. I am on medication and I don't think I can do anything," I whine.

"Yes you can. Let's start with something easy."

She brings me a hook, colored wool and a large cloth that looks like burlap. Then she explains what to do.

First I have to draw, in pencil, a design or a picture on the burlap. I draw a little house, a tree, a fence, a lawn, a path, a sky, and clouds. Exactly the same picture I drew when I was still alive. It is impossible for me to think of something new.

Then I start the hooking. It is difficult. It takes me ages to thread the wool. It is also hard to push the hook right through the burlap, to fish for a new strand, and coax it upward through the hole.

I get exasperated and humiliate myself by asking the teacher for something still easier.

I end up making pot holders. I take the wool and needle to the ward and make one after the other so as not to have to think. Life has gone out of me. I get no treatment beside the Thorazine, hook therapy, watch bowling, and the like. Dr. Dalton speaks to me from time to time, right on the ward in everybody's presence, for five minutes. I tell him, "I felt so good, but since I started Thorazine I am depressed and barely living."

"Your ward behavior surely has improved," he remarks casually.

Now I understand! The antischizophrenic drugs are meant to cure you, not by making you happy, creative and loving, but by making you tractable. The hospital is satisfied, since sitting in a rocking chair and making pot holders is a sure way of avoiding trouble.

And soon, the doctors think, I will be able to live in the community, where, filled with Thorazine, I can score tests and compute IQ's instead of reenacting the Revolutionary War.

My Jesus delusion is gradually fading. The other patients are just patients, not figures from the gospel; and the beautiful woman whom I called Maria because I thought she would play Jesus' mother is just a housewife from Fort Wayne named Edna.

But within me is still a glowing sun, now buried and invisible, waiting for the moment to erupt and shine. Perhaps the Thorazine does more than change you into a robot. Perhaps it gives you rest to heal inside until it's time, until it's time.

The flock of geese (of which I am one) goes to the snack bar several times a week. So do the doctors, nurses, aides, et cetera, et cetera. Patients stand in long lines to get coffee, soft drinks, milk shakes, candy or toothpaste. The staff lines up in shorter lines. Then we sit around heavy tables, patients with patients, doctors with doctors, aides with aides, except that one aide sits at every patients' table.

I don't like candy bars, milk shakes, soft drinks or coffee, and if I would buy toothpaste every time it would be viewed as a perversion. I do force down some gooey stuff so that my chart won't say REFUSES SNACK.

One day I sit at a table alone with my required Hershey bar, expecting other patients and an aide to join me. Then something unexpected happens. Dr. Sorcy joins me. He is the counterculture doctor who spoke on my behalf during the trial.

"How are you, Dr. Joelson?" He is the only one who calls me doctor.

"I am much better since you spoke during the staff meeting. Did you get flack?"

He smiles. "Oh yes. But does it matter?"

And now both of us smile.

Since Tobey left there has not been a flow of love between another person and myself (except my ex-husband, some students and some colleagues).

"What a glorious *vision* to play the role of Christ!" says Dr. Sorcy.

The tears stream from my eyes, and Dr. Sorcy says quickly, "Let's change seats."

Now I face the wall and he the snack shop. No one can see me cry. I use my napkin so as not to dig into my bra in Dr. Sorcy's presence. Finally I recover my composure, and a flash of that familiar high zigzags through me. Sorcy and Joelson versus Thorazine.

And like a fish back in the water, I want to tell him, tell him, tell him about the wonders I have seen.

I start excitedly, "Everyone thinks it is so dreadful to have hallucinations or—as you call them—visions. But it is one of the most beautiful gifts I ever received—the gift to see the world quite differently than I saw it all my life—I couldn't believe that such transfigurations really happen."

Dr. Sorcy does not say anything, instead he laughs and laughs and laughs. He does not laugh about me. He seems to laugh as if something obvious, hidden for centuries, has suddenly come to light.

Then he seems to speak more to himself than to me: "It was like a miracle. You could transform the world in which we live into a passion

114

play. You walked on the streets of a small Midwestern town and transfigured it into holy ground. As it were, you walked where Christ walked 2,000 years ago."

"But why that horror in the faces of people at St. Mary when I told them?"

"Your rapture is not accepted in the world in which we live. You know that Faulkner wrote, 'Craziness ain't so much what a fellow does, but it's the way the majority of folks is looking at him when he does it.'"

I interrupt, "Oh yes, of course!"

"And then we cured you. Now a small Midwestern town is just a small Midwestern town and nothing more."

"Yes, the world is cold and empty."

He whispers consolingly: "But you'll recover! Then you will not want to transform the world into a passion play, but you will have moments when you can look at the real world with rapture, when everything around you becomes enthralled and glorious. There'll still be many mysteries for you to solve."

I venture, "Perhaps my 'vision' was not a breakdown but a breakthrough?"

And he says weightily, "Oh yes, perhaps it was."

Then I complain, "I felt so holy, but now I'm told it's a disease."

"It doesn't matter what you call it. I studied your transfigurations of reality quite thoroughly. You have a longing for oneness. At Valley View *every single thing* had to fit your notion that people wanted *money* from you. Even Tobey, whom you loved dearly, became suspect. Then the patients' poverty and your wealth vanished completely from your mind, and every single thing was caused by *pills*. And later, at St. Mary, you were not satisfied until the convent, the town and the entire world had one prime mover: *Christ*, reenacted by yourself. You must be nostalgic for the centuries when everybody believed in one prime mover, in Providence."

I am intrigued. "How come you are so different from all these doctors?"

He blushes and explains, "I took a class which made me see the world of mental illness in a new light."

I ask with great surprise, "A class?"

"Yes, I took a class."

"A class in medical school?"

He shakes his head.

"Then where?"

"In the Department of Psychology."

I am almost too surprised to speak. "Psychology? But where?"

"In Indiana, at Purdue University."

My heart pounds heavily. "What class was it, what was the name?"

He whispers, "Abnormal psychology taught by Dr. Joelson."

My lips begin to tremble.

He fumbles for his wallet and fingers awkwardly until he finds a photograph. He hands me the picture over the table and explains, "This is how I looked without a beard and with short hair."

I exclaim, "Tom, is it really you?"

He answers with tears in his voice, "Yes, Dr. Joelson."

Then we walk silently back to the flock, the two of us, once teacher and student, now student and teacher. He says, "So long," and I sit down to finish my pot holder before we go to supper.

Today something incredible happened: I was called to the telephone. It raised my status enormously that someone from the outside world wanted to talk to me—not to my doctor, no, to me in person.

Dream Reader, I'd like to blurt it out immediately and tell you who it was, but there is something that you have to know so you will understand. When I found out that I was to play the role of Christ, I resigned from my tenured position as a full professor at Purdue, where I had worked for about eleven years with utmost dedication. Who wants to work at some old school if she can travel with a passion show from town to town, from state to state as Jesus Christ, the Lord Himself?

I hold the receiver to my ear with my right hand, clenching the pot holder in my left fist.

"This is Dr. _____ , chairman of psychology at Duke University. We would like to offer you a position as a visiting professor at Duke for this next school year beginning in September." (It is late July.)

I say with trembling voice, "I can't decide so quickly."

"We have to know by August 10."

"I'll get back to you," I stammer.

"Fine."

Now I am sitting on a bench, speechless and numb. What if the doctors won't permit it? If they will keep me imprisoned in this Thorazine bar? Might it be better not to tell them now and try my best to speed up my recovery? Then on August 10, I shall face my judges and demand my freedom. And this is what I decide to do.

Next morning, after breakfast, I try to write my journal again. But Thorazine does not approve; it holds the still unfinished pot holder before my eyes. Mazie agrees with Thorazine and says, "Finish your pretty pot holder, Miz Joelson. Mrs. Fender will be here at 9:00 and bring new wool in different colors to make another one."

"Yes," I yawn. But I know that sweet Mazie's mind wanders far and fast and she will never notice if I don't finish the execrated pot holder.

Thus I get some paper and an envelope from the unknown aide who guards the counter and write:

> To: Dr. Tom Sorcy
> From: Edith Joelson
> *When I was mad I flooded the outer world with my inner life until the world disappeared and everything became dream, wish, and fantasy. But if the mad person does not become too fearful of this ocean of inner life, she will be able to withdraw the flood slowly and lovingly and see the earth again, an earth which is no longer withered and dry, an earth which is now bathed in the nectar of the human soul.*

Now the reply:

> To: Dr. Edith Joelson
> From: Tom Sorcy
> *Yes. I agree.*
> *Therefore you must get well. You have a lot to do. You have to teach and write. Those who go into madness and are able to return from it bring treasures with them which they must share.*
> *Withdraw the flood and see the earth again!*

My life has changed so much. I know I'll soon be well.

117

A few days later I sit again with Hershey bar and much anticipation in the snack room at an empty table. Soon Dr. Sorcy joins me saying he has spoken with Dr. Dalton, who has agreed to let him work with me under supervision on little projects.

"Stop all this silly stuff—pot holders and hooked rugs and whatnot. What do you really want to do?"

"To play the role of Christ in a passion play."

"Then play the role of Christ."

"But how?"

"What is it about Christ you want to emulate?"

"He was a teacher and a preacher and said things to people which are true and cleansing."

"Then teach and preach."

"Here on the ward?"

"No, not here on the ward. But isn't writing a form of teaching, too?"

"Yes, but the Thorazine . . . ."

"Oh, you are stronger than the Thorazine. You wrote a beautiful little essay just a few days ago."

I gave in and started to write. One paragraph or two a day, then I got scared and tired. It took me sixteen days to write what I needed to say. When I finished, I sealed the manuscript and sent it to Dr. Sorcy.[1]

I was released from Pineville Mental Hospital in time to start teaching in the fall semester of 1966 at Duke University.

---

[1] The text of Dr. Weisskopf-Joelson's manuscript is printed in the Appendix.

My Harvest
after Madness

Tomorrow is Thanksgiving, the day when our colonial forebears celebrated the harvest which they had reaped from a strenuous year of tilling the soil. This is a good day to write about my own harvest, which I have reaped from a strenuous episode of madness.

First, let me tell you about the external events which happened after I was discharged from the mental hospital. I was never told what my diagnosis was when I was discharged, but from my knowledge of psychology I assumed that at that time (1966) it must have been something like "paranoid schizophrenia in remission."

"Paranoid" meant that I had delusions, a word which was defined as follows: "A firm belief opposed to reality but maintained in spite of strong evidence to the contrary."

"Schizophrenia" meant "a psychosis characterized by the breakdown of integrated personality functioning, withdrawal from reality, emotional blunting and distortion, and disturbances in thought and behavior."

And "in remission" meant that I was still sick, but that my sickness had gone "underground" for the time being. Since I still possessed this sickness, however, it was quite possible that it might come to the surface again.

This brief discussion of my "official" diagnostic label does not mean that I accept the label and the stigma attached to it. If I am a schizophrenic "in remission," then almost all of us who do not suffer from the common cold on this day could be labeled as suffering from "a common cold in remission," since almost all of us have had a common cold in the past and will, most likely, have one again in the future. But "in remission" implies the unproven assumption that the disease is still within me, even though it cannot be seen or felt in any part of me.

That much about my diagnosis. Towards the second half of my stay at the mental hospital, I became worried about what I would do after my discharge. I was separated from my husband and did not feel I could return to his house just for convenience's sake. I had resigned from my tenured position (a tenured academic position is a position which the employer cannot terminate until the employee has reached mandatory retirement age) as full professor of psychology at Purdue University. My retirement letter was written during my spiritual delusion when I thought that the years to come would be taken up with my work as an actress playing the role of Jesus. (Several comments in my diary indicate that I anticipated the passion play would not be a one-time performance only. Instead I expected that we would be a travelling theatrical group, giving performances all over this country and possibly even in other countries.) But since I no longer believed in the reality of this role, I had to look for another position, preferably a position of the same kind as the one I had held before I became mad.[1] I wrote many letters to let it be known that I was available. Finally I was called to the telephone by the head nurse of the mental hospital: to my amazement, the Psychology Department of Duke, one of the best universities in this country, offered me a visiting professorship for one year. I accepted the offer and did a fairly good job for one year. At the end of that year, I was offered a more permanent position at the University of Georgia, where I remained for eleven years as a professor of psychology and, during the last few months, as a retired part-time professor (professor emerita), still teaching and participating in the activities of the university.[2]

During my years in Georgia, I became a different person than I had been before. A better person in my own eyes and in the eyes of those close to me. At the age of fifty-seven, I found myself changing and growing like an adolescent. I ascribed much of this growth to my journey

---

[1]The author's brother, Dr. Walter Weisskopf, recalls that his sister told him in a telephone conversation before her release from Pineville that she was not ready for a conventional existence. She would be able to return to her teaching position at Purdue because her letter of resignation was written while mentally ill, but she said she was looking forward to enjoying her freedom. It is not clear why she seemed to have changed her mind and applied to other universities for a teaching position.

[2]This was written in 1978. Dr. Weisskopf-Joelson kept teaching as a retired part-time professor until her death in 1983.

through madness. Thus, I decided to think of my madness not as a breakdown but as a breakthrough.

I shall try to lead you through some of the changes which I have observed in myself. In no case did I *intend* to change, but the change occurred without my own volition, and frequently I noticed the change only after it had occurred.

I no longer attempted to impersonate a "normal" person, whereas in my earlier life I wanted to be normal even if it killed me.

There are so many things which others can do without much effort and which I can do only with utmost strain. It is hard for me to keep an apartment or a house clean and neat, to give a dinner party, to do many things at the same time. I cannot be a woman who works *creatively* from eight to five (how can one limit one's creative outpour to specific hours?), who then picks up two preschool children from two different places, goes home and fixes dinner, washes the dishes and then changes into a glamorous creature (no mascara dripping down the cheeks, no runner in the pantyhose) for the evening cocktail party, and who, while doing all of this, shows interest in her husband and her children. Not being able to accomplish this would be deficient only if I *wanted* to live this way. But no, I do not, and if I did, it would be only because I wanted to be like others.

Thus, I decided that impersonation of someone I am not is immoral and a waste of time.

I live alone and like it and have many friends. I won't remarry unless a miracle occurs. My place—two rooms—is messy when I am alone and reaches borderline acceptability when others are expected.

Instead of despairing that other people can do so much that I cannot do, I ask myself what it is that I *can* do. For there are tasks that only I can do or only a few can do, and therefore, I *must* do them. If not I, then who?

What is it, then, that I can do? I feel that God has given me the courage to speak up and say what I believe, even though my beliefs may be opposed to the beliefs of others. I feel that God has given me a sensitivity— others may call it a sickness—which makes me suffer when something goes astray in my environment. He also has given me the talent to mold my suffering like the sculptor molds the clay, to mold it into a thing of beauty and of passion. To tell others about my suffering until they feel their own suffering about that which has gone astray and try to alter it. What are these things that have gone astray and make me suffer?

Much of psychology has become a desert where *mind* and *soul* and *consciousness* are unscientific words. Behavior is the only idol to be studied. If you behave as if you loved, you love. I cannot live with such a view of life. I am greatly influenced by Viktor Frankl's philosophy of life. Also, much of psychotherapy has become adjustment to society; the gentle man who loves good poetry is given training in assertiveness, and the proud and forceful woman who defends her equal rights to justice is given training in surrender.

The idealistic graduate student in clinical psychology, aware that we know little about the mentally ill or how to help them, is trained to be a professional man or woman in a gray flannel suit who speaks with great authority on things we do not know. Then, when a faculty meets and judges students, and puts them on parole or drops them from the program for "sins" like being late or cancelling some appointments, those who are themselves so full of "sins" cast stones without remorse.

I have made it my own task to stand up in front of learned men and women and tell them whenever they have gone astray. I have replaced adjustment with protest. But not protest in hate, instead protest in love. Now I begin to understand my spiritual delusion: it was not really a delusion; instead, it told me what I am meant to do—to play the role of Christ, not in a passion play, but in *real* life. The role of Christ has many facets, but one, it seems, is better suited to my life than all the others: Christ was a revolutionary on earth, an "I-say-unto-you" man, as I like to call him. He stated more than once: "Ye have heard that . . . . But I say unto you . . . ." And then he preached something quite different from what the mainstream of society believed.

There are many other "I-say-unto-you" men and women, like Martin Luther, Mahatma Gandhi, Martin Luther King, Jr., and Susan B. Anthony. None as great as Christ, but they were Christ-like. And in a very, very small way, I have become an "I-say-unto-you" woman as well. I have become one through a message that I received when I was mad. Can madness, then, be the dread disease we think it is?

The harvest from my madness gave me many other new thoughts. It made me wonder whether madness and minor forms of maladjustment may not be signposts toward a mission which gives life its meaning. And since, during my lifetime, I was mad at one time and maladjusted to a less serious degree at other times, and since I am also a psychologist, I feel that it is my duty to teach and write about the mission of the maladjusted.

We are being forced into a mode of life which violates our basic nature. We are not meant to be efficient and speedy from morning to night, without time and opportunity to contemplate, fantasize, dream, feel, and experience. Those who are able to violate their nature and to function solely according to the demands of the external world, those are the well adjusted. Those who cannot do so are the maladjusted. They are the people who cannot be oppressed, the people who cannot bear the cold rationality of a scientific age, the people who refuse to be converted into machines, the people whose inner lives are too strong and incorruptible to permit smooth functioning in a mass society. The number of maladjusted people is becoming larger and larger. Soon it will be large enough to be of political significance in changing an inhuman society into a human one.

But the mission of maladjusted people is not only a collective one; it is also an individual one. Being maladjusted may, at times, give us the obligation to keep our maladjustment alive and to set an example for others. Those among us who always present a smooth, poised, well-groomed and well-adjusted facade are often a damaging influence for others. They make the rest of us feel as if we had a hole in our stocking or a spot on our tie. In contrast, there is nothing more liberating and more growth producing than to see a person who does not quite fit in—who openly displays humanness and inability to function smoothly. It permits observers to loosen their own controls and to say: "It is all right to be different!"

Our maladjustment may become meaningful if we do not conform, if we do not adjust, if we remain true to ourselves. Our maladjustment may become meaningful if we speak to others about our pain, if we speak to others about our hunger for the many things which are missing not only in *our* lives, but also in *their* lives and in the lives of many contemporary men and women. Already sensitive people are getting together in groups to talk about their lives in an overly rational, mechanical and materialistic society. More and more groups of this kind are emerging, islands of growth in the midst of a barren field. These islands will grow and multiply until they cease to be islands, until they become a solid field, a new field of hope covering the old field of despair. It is the maladjusted who may bring about a better world.

Maladjustment is often accompanied by suffering. Before we realize that our maladjustment might be our most valuable uniqueness, we may have to suffer, both in the belief that we really are inferior and in the painful attempt to adjust. Even after we have understood our mission, we will find it painful to live in a world so ill-fitted to our needs. The pain of "misfits" is eminently meaningful. It is a pain which will grow and grow until it becomes powerful enough to bring about the birth of a new era, an era of human wholeness and fulfillment.

If mental illness is not an illness in the traditional sense of the word, but a condition that can be viewed as good or bad, then those who have experienced the positive aspects of madness have an important task to fulfill, namely, to change the image of the mad person in the eyes of the public. Blacks and women have made a united effort in this direction with regard to their own minorities. Why could those who have experienced madness not do the same? (A start has already been made to move in this direction.)

It is hoped that this book may represent one step toward this goal, that it may give the reader a glimpse of the mysterious beauty, the terror, the sadness, and the healing rebirth brought into existence by the strange experience which we call madness.

The Meaning of My Illness

This was to be the end of my report about my lonely voyage. I put the diary into a locked safe without intending to ever take it out again. But on this day I took my writings out of their seclusion and reread them. My life, I feel, has been a very rich one but not comfortable. It has been full of tragedies and pain, but every tragedy has contributed to further growth. This was especially true for the one "tragedy" through which we travelled together in this book. But only after I emerged from the flood of madness could I see new meaning in my life. I have not only studied madness, as other students of psychology have done, but also lived through it. This coexistence of knowledge and experience presents a mandate I must fulfill, that I have already partially fulfilled when attempting to teach my students about madness.

Now I must do more. I have arrived at the point of my "crucifixion." No, I do not believe that I must play the role of Christ. But—if I may be permitted to compare the big with the small—is not the awesome crucifixion of Christ a symbol of our personal and much more trivial "crucifixion"?

It may well be that one of my crucifixions is the publication of this book. I shall have to walk among my students who admire and love me, among colleagues who respect me, among friends who enjoy me, and all will know that I was mad. Those who view former mental patients with fear and contempt will remember how much they liked to be with me before they knew. And then perhaps we all will wonder if madness is not something quite different from what it appears.

129

In the late 1950s when I read psychoanalytical books, the realization came to me as to what caused madness. (Although no one knows what causes schizophrenia, almost all European experts think it is an organic disease, a biochemical imbalance.) But when I read these books, I felt that my sickness had its roots in my unconscious belief that I killed my father by not loving him. He remained a stranger in his family, but he loved me passionately. I was his only link to his family, and I could not return his love. He was so proud of me! When we walked through the parks and streets of Vienna, he would stop his friends (he seemed to know half of Vienna) and say, "This is *my* little girl. She is only eleven and can already read Latin," and he would give me the most loving look I had ever received. Zuzu looked at me a bit like Father did, but my relationship to Vati was not childlike, as the one to Zuzu was. On the contrary, when I was as young as nine, Father treated me as if I were an adult judge and presented me with real or fictitious court problems. At sixteen, by his deathbed, I dried the perspiration from his face continuously, and he said, "I would not permit anybody to do this, only my little daughter." I realized later he meant to tell me that I was his only tie to the family.

I loved him when he was gone during World War I. But I never forgot his homecoming as a Polish Jew peddler, because his behavior after this and until his death reminded me of his inferior status. Inferior? He was among the foremost attorneys in Vienna, but his *origin* was low in the eyes of Mother. Vati wanted me to know a little about Judaism and once asked a clerk in his office to invite me to a Seder. Father came to pick me up. He took the bowl of chopped apples, nuts, and raisins, which symbolized the freeing of the Jews from Egypt, and ate it with the spoon that was in the bowl. I was embarrassed because the bowl was supposed to be a serving bowl, and you were to take one spoonful and put it on your plate.

There were many such incidents. In the morning he would leave the door open between my room and the bedroom he and Mother shared. While he dressed, he would pace the floor and hum. Humming was a sign that he was thinking about his forthcoming address in court. But when he paced, his suspenders were down, and his pants would come down so that I could see his underwear. I thought he looked ridiculous.

Father died of pleurisy. I had pleurisy, too, at the age of nine. I had inherited his disposition to respiratory illnesses, including TB. I don't blame him for this; on the contrary, I think this is something I have to remember him by. The doctor said that his heart was weakened by World War I and the Russian prisoner-of-war camp, but I know that if I had shown him the utmost tender love, he would not have died then.

During the later years in Vienna, I was charitable toward the poor. The poor represented Father. Before that, when I was about nine, I behaved strangely. I prayed to God, which we were never taught to do. I prayed because I felt guilty for looking down on Father. I prayed for forgiveness, but didn't tell anybody. Mother would have viewed it as a psychopathological symptom.

All this is connected to my delusions. They were economic, biochemical, and spiritual. The economic delusion represented a small redemption of my lack of love for Father. If it were really true that everybody was after my money, I could get redemption by giving to the poor, who represented my father. And I did give quite a bit. My delusion said symbolically: "Father asks for love. I can't give him love. Money stands for love. If I give money to the poor, who represent Father, I will be redeemed."

The biochemical delusion was also a wish fulfillment. My guilt lay heavily upon my shoulders, and psychedelic drugs are an effective way of escaping. If one takes drugs in a supervised experiment, there is no need for guilt.

The spiritual delusion: Christ washes away all our sins. His crucifixion makes us free of sins. Thus, when I play the role of Christ, I am free of sins and help others to be free of sins. The problems of my life are solved: I have become a redeemer and the redeemed. And I can say, as Christ, to my Father in Heaven: "Forgive me, Father, for I knew not that I killed my earthly father."

Today my views of these delusions have broadened from an analytical to an existential interpretation.

Economic

As I look back at my economic interpretation, I find that it can hardly be called a delusion. While it happens rarely that one principle suffices to explain even the small world of a tuberculosis ward, the economic inequality between my fellow patients and myself was so drastic that it was, in all probability, the main factor which governed our relationship. Perhaps it would have been more delusional to assume that pure love and friendship, untainted by material considerations, could have developed between me and the other patients.

Yet, even though my interpretation was largely correct, my thirst for oneness led to some explanations which I now consider incorrect. For example, my view that Tobey's approach towards me was brought about altogether by financial considerations on the part of his parents does not seem convincing in retrospect, even though such considerations might have been partially responsible for his interest in me.

As I look back upon this strange period of my life, it also strikes me that my delusions—the small delusion which I have reported and the more drastic ones which I am about to report—have much in common with the manner in which many scholars interpret the world. My economic interpretation, for example, has something in common with Karl Marx's interpretation of history, an interpretation which is exclusively based on economic factors. It seems that the desire to find a single principle which could take the place of Providence can be found in scholars, as well as in confused individuals who cannot accept the complexity of the world which surrounds them.

Furthermore, an answer to why one of my delusions was economic seems to be buried in my past. From the time I was born to the time when Hitler relieved me of my money, I viewed myself as wealthy in a land of poverty and malnutrition, and I felt guilty.

It was hard to be a "have" among the "have-nots." World War I raged when I was between the ages of four and eight. Being among the wealthy few was a central theme which orchestrated much of my early life. Later, when young men dated me and then suggested marriage, my friends or family would question whether my suitor's love was genuine or whether he wanted to marry me for money and social status.

Thus, it is not surprising that I developed an economic delusion. In the tuberculosis hospital, I was rich among the poor and was approached for money rather than for love. But I magnified the pain and the scope of the deception by "adding" all the pains and deceptions of this kind which I had experienced in my youth.

Biochemical

My second interpretation of the ambiguous situation in which I found myself was a biochemical one—not unlike the interpretations given by many scholars who hold that biochemical processes are the main factors determining human behavior.

Viewing my interpretation retrospectively, I have reached the conclusion that it was *mostly* delusional. The place in which I found myself was truly a hospital for pulmonary diseases. It was not a place in which experiments on psychotropic drugs were conducted. However, as is usually the case, my interpretation was not entirely delusional; instead, it contained some realistic elements. Most of the patients, including myself, were taking antituberculosis drugs, some of which have considerable psychological side effects. In addition, various sedatives and antidepressants were administered to most patients, including myself, in order to ease the discomfort and impatience caused by prolonged bedrest and inactivity. The purpose of all medication was the treatment of pulmonary diseases rather than psychological experimentation.

I had tried to interpret my *whole* world first on the basis of an economic principle, then on the basis of a biochemical principle. In both cases I had erred. As my biochemical pattern faded and finally fell apart, I was wondering what my next worldview would turn out to be.

Spiritual

My third interpretation of the changed and ambiguous situation in which I found myself was a spiritual one.

Firstly, I was brought up without religion and without a God. There was a time when I made up my own God and prayed to Him with feeling and passion. (I must have been between the ages of seven and nine.) It was considered moving by my father, but not so by my mother: praying to her was low-brow, inelegant, and mildly crazy.

Much earlier when I was between three and five, religion was for me what sex was for the other children. It was secret and forbidden, and I was punished for exploring it. And that is how religion became secret, exciting and forbidden in my childhood.

Viewing my interpretation retrospectively, I must of course come to the conclusion that it was totally delusional. Those at the college of St. Mary did not plan to perform a passion play, and even if they had, I would hardly have been selected for the role of Jesus Christ.

However, even a delusion as blatant as the one which I created is meaningful if properly interpreted. Viktor E. Frankl, the author of *Man's Search for Meaning,* interprets human existence as a search for a purpose, a goal, a reason for living. Without such meaning we live in an "existential vacuum," a condition which, while painful, is likely to cause us to spurn our search for something or somebody to live for.

My own existential vacuum was symbolized by my empty mailbox on Obedience Day when the sisters were given their mission for the coming year. It was also symbolized by my visit to the cemetery which seemed to say that there was nothing for me to do but wait for death. After my long stay in the tuberculosis hospital, I was looking for new meaning and for reaffirmation of the old meaning which my life had before my illness. This search led me to the seemingly bizarre conclusion that it was the purpose of my life at St. Mary to play the role of Christ in a passion play. This conclusion is bizarre only if it is perceived literally instead of metaphorically, just as a dream is bizarre if it is accepted at face value. Sigmund Freud distinguishes between the manifest dream content and the latent dream thought: the former is the actual dream as remembered by the dreamer, while the latter is the meaning of the dream after it has been decoded and interpreted. Similarly, a delusion might correspond to the manifest dream content and might require interpretation just as a dream does.

The figure of Jesus Christ has been symbolically interpreted according to many schools of thought, but whenever I try to apply any of these interpretations to my own experience, whenever I try to analyze the great mystery which entered my life in the form of a delusion, I find that I destroy it. The act of analysis is an act of dissection, and I wish to keep my mystery untouched and whole. Thus, let me just say that the story of Christ's life could not have inspired humankind for centuries if it did not symbolize human existence in a multitude of ways—if it did not touch upon our faint awareness that we must die to be reborn, on our longing to find meaning in our suffering, on our belief that power destroys but humility nourishes, and above all, on our passionate yearning for immortality.

My delusion carried meaning, a meaning too close and too sacred to be put into words. The effects of this "message without words" is strong and bright and visible. I have come out of my madness with a strong feeling of purpose and identity. I also have the strong desire to communicate with others who have had similar experiences, to communicate especially the fact that madness—one of the most dreaded experiences in human life—can also be full of ecstasy. I ask, again and again, the questions so forcefully worded by John Weir Perry when he wrote:

Do we have the right any longer to regard madness as mere mental disease and disorder? For what, then, would we make of the fact that some people emerge from such an episode weller than well, as one psychiatrist has put it? That is, some come out of this state with a newly quickened capacity for depth in their concerns, their callings, and their relationships. What do we make of the fact that when out of their senses, some people have experiences perhaps of beauty, perhaps of terror, but always with implications of awesome depth, and that when they reemerge out of their craze and into their so-called normal ego, they may shut the trapdoor after them and close out their vision once more and become prosaic in the extreme, straightened in a bland and shallow usualness? What goes wrong when someone becomes a visionary, looking into the heart of his cosmos and of his fellow beings around him, only when he is sick, only to become blind, constricted, and timid, understanding nothing, when he is well again, dependent for the rest of his days perhaps on a drug to keep his soul and its vision dampened down and safely out of reach?

The break with "reality" which I undertook is regarded as one of the most dreadful experiences which can happen to a human being. But if I were asked to name one of the most beautiful gifts which I have received during my lifetime, I would say it was the gift of being able to transform the prosaic world in which we live into the scene of a great passion play. I walked on the streets of a small Midwestern town and transformed it into holy ground, as it were. I walked where Christ walked 2,000 years ago. Only when I saw the horror in the faces of those to whom I disclosed myself did I realize that my rapture was not acceptable to the world in which I lived. Then they cured me, and my rapture

135

was killed by drugs. Thereafter, as Tom Sorcy had put it, a small Midwestern town was just a small Midwestern town and nothing more. The world was cold and empty.

Now I have recovered. I can no longer transform the earth into a passion play, but I still have moments when I look at the world with rapture, when everything around me becomes enthralled and glorious. I still have moments when I feel there is a mystery surrounding me which I must solve.

When I was mad I flooded the outer world with my inner life until the world disappeared and everything became dream, wish, and fantasy. But if the mad person does not become too fearful of this ocean of inner life, she will be able to withdraw the flood slowly and lovingly and see the earth again, an earth which is no longer withered and dry, an earth which is now bathed in the nectar of the human soul.

Afterword

Viktor Frankl

To any unbiased and unprejudiced reader, the account that Edith gives of her experiences makes for a great and deep experience on his part as well. To me, it was gripping and moving, and I could not help but be reminded of the best-selling old-timer *Lost Horizon* by James Hilton. For there, too, we are introduced to a world of its own, far away—and above—our world of routine and trivialities; instead, we are shown a way of life that allows for contemplation and meditation and the inner enrichment deriving therefrom. But we also are shown the abysmal despair that accompanies anyone who chooses to return from the spiritual heights and peaks to the depth of the valleys. This condition has been described by many a mystic, after the bliss of ecstasy, as a dreadful state of continuing inner emptiness: and they called it "the dark night of the soul."

What Edith has experienced, however, is not solely a matter to which one may respond emotionally or react intellectually, and the way in which she narrates it is not only apt to evoke all the empathy of which one can dispose; what we have to admire first and foremost is her courage bluntly to confront us with the facts. In disclosing them, Edith offers a huge sacrifice on the altar of many who underwent similar stirring experiences and now, rather than feeling ashamed or mentally crippled, may learn how to turn the negative into something positive, tragedy into a triumph, a predicament into an achievement on the human level.

This does not at all detract from the fact that I cannot subscribe to the more theoretical inferences at which Edith arrives, namely that paranoia is caused by the need for a comprehensive meaning. I, for one,

137

have the conviction that the primary origin of the condition Edith calls "madness" is of some biochemical nature, even though more often than not its exact nature could not yet be determined and identified. To a member of the medical profession, this is no strange state of affairs. How many among the diseases confronting the physician are of an unknown origin? Just consider cancer.

However, what the experiencing person makes of it is entirely the property of his human personality. The "madness" that afflicts him is biochemical. But how he adopts it, how he reacts to it, what he invests into it, the content with which he fills in the mold—all this is his personal creation, the human work into which he has molded his experience.

Edith was right in linking her story to logotherapy's concept of "meaning in suffering." As I see it, however, "madness" is not meaningful by itself but may only become meaningful—may only be endowed with meaning—by what one does about it, by the remaining and enduring inner growth one reaps from it. In other words, "viewing mental illness in a more positive light," as Edith puts it, is all okay. But this positive light, rather than being shed by the interpretations of an analyst, is irradiating and emanating from the spiritual core of the experiencing person. It bears witness of what I call "the defiant power of the human spirit."

A last word be granted to me concerning Edith's conviction that one has to bear the "cross" of life's meaninglessness—that after one has recovered and then been thrown into "the dark night of the soul," one is condemned again to listen to "the tale told by an idiot" to the effect that life "signifies nothing." I do not believe that this is what we have to bear—the meaninglessness of life. What we really have to bear is our human incapacity to grasp the infinite meaningfulness of life in merely intellectual terms. "The more comprehensive the meaning is," I once said, "the less comprehensible it is." Therefore, ultimate meaning eludes any attempt to get hold of it on purely rational grounds. We do not have to cope with meaninglessness, only with our own helplessness *vis-à*-vis ultimate meaning. It is in no way justified to deny the very possibility of such meaning. For, upon closer investigation, any such denial is based on merely a priori assumptions. There are even indications that in the depth of their being, all persons believe in ultimate meaning.

138

Appendix

A Letter to My
Unborn Schizophrenic Son

My Dear,

After daydreaming much about you, I finally decided not to conceive you. This decision occurred a long time ago, when I was still young enough to bear children.

Today I should like to speak to you, my unborn son. I should like to explain to you why you are unborn. I should also like to tell you today, my dear unborn child, how I have experienced a gradual changing of heart and I wish, at last, you had come into the world.

I made my decision not to give birth to you because I was a different kind of person and feared that I would pass my genes of differentness onto you. I feared you would be born "schizophrenic." My expectation of such a dreadful tragedy, as many would perceive it, was based on two considerations.

First, there is some evidence that a disposition to become schizophrenic can be hereditary. I began to notice at a very early age that I was unusual in many ways. This observation persisted into adulthood and is still with me today during this summer evening which I am spending with you. When I started to study psychology, I began to realize that an overwhelming number of these differences between myself and others were warning signals of schizophrenia. My suspicion did not prove unfounded since later, at the age of fifty-two, I did suffer what psychology calls a "schizophrenic episode."

I also began to recognize that these differences could make me the kind of mother who, I have read, allegedly contributes to the develop-

141

ment of a schizoid personality in her child. Thus, I decided not to pass on to you genes that might have channeled your life in a direction which society and the world have called "evil" and "ill" as a condemnation without the possibility of redemption.

Today, as a mature woman, I ask myself, What is good and what is evil? Would you now call schizoid evil or ill? I would not. Who is to say what is healthy and what is sick? As a student I gullibly accepted the words of my professors, physicians, and the books I read, as the final authority on these matters. But now I wonder if all these learned people have considered asking "evil" and "ill" people why they find it so difficult to understand their differentness. The schizophrenics' way of looking at life, the objects and goals they value, the styles in which they live, differ from those professors, physicians, and authors—the mainstream people in society—to such an extent that the two species just cannot understand each other.

When I was an adolescent, I valued the aspects of my personality which resembled those of others, while I was ashamed of and tried to hide the aspects of myself which did not conform to the norms. Only now, in my fifties, do I recognize that often those parts of ourselves which distinguish us from others are the ones which help us find the unique roles we are meant to play in life. I now believe, my unborn son, you would have been a unique person in this difficult world in which you would have lived.

What would you have been like if you had been born? For one thing, you would have been a "stranger" to life, a schizophrenic among so-called normals. There are so many different societies—an inhabitant of the United States who is liked by his peers would be considered quite odd among a tribe living off the shore of eastern New Guinea.

The degrading term "schizophrenic" makes it difficult to consider that we may be of some use to society. Therefore, why not call ourselves Strangers? Then we would call normal people, to whom the mainstream of society seems to be their oyster, Natives.

Strangers and Natives do not represent two separate groups. Instead, they represent a continuum of people, most of whom possess characteristics of both kinds—of both Natives and Strangers. It is for didactic reasons only that I am speaking of Natives and Strangers as two separate groups rather than as points on a continuum.

Those Natives have much to say about us Strangers, especially those Natives whom society has told to label us, study us, explain us, care for us, and use us.

While many of us are popular, friendly and sociable, we find it difficult to form truly intimate and lasting relationships with others. Perhaps those who judge us are trying to say that we cannot love. Many of us Strangers can "love" quite well. Many of us are sexually and emotionally skillful and competent. But they say we cannot love. This accusation hurts me most. For it is impossible to interact with Natives without noticing that emotionally intimate human relations are one of the things that keeps them alive. Thus, in this respect your life would have been a hard one. Unless you were a handsome and intelligent young man, your distant, foggy look would have challenged others to get close to you, to love you, and teach you how to love.

Strangers can love intensely, even if it is a "love" Natives call "immature" and "inconsequential." These Natives don't understand that we Strangers have an overwhelming ability to develop a kind of love which might be called infatuation. We become easily infatuated with individuals whose private lives are mostly unfamiliar to us and then can be filled with our own dreams. Teachers, actors, and athletes are those public personalities we will often become infatuated with.

We also become infatuated with our psychotherapists. And we "sick" Strangers often find ourselves under their care. Sigmund Freud called the love of patient for therapist "transference" and predicted we Strangers could not be analyzed because we are too narcissistic, or self-loving, to enter into this necessary and beneficial transference. We now know that Freud was mistaken. We "fall in love" with our therapists all the time. In fact, many Strangers need to worship someone who does not quite exist in our reality, someone who is half-known and half-unknown, half-real and half-dream.

We Strangers have converted psychotherapy into something quite creative to our existence—something it was not originally meant to do. While less unusual patients might undergo therapy to help them live more fully outside the therapy situation, many Strangers find that the psychotherapeutic session itself becomes their whole reason for living. When they get the first taste of a transference relationship, they realize immediately that this is the elixir which they have been yearning for all their lives. And their lives become acceptable, happy, even blissful when they bring the fantasy figure of the therapist into their personal lives. And now it does not matter anymore whether life's realities are dull or bright, for there is always a presence which transfigures their world into a place of enchantment. Thus, many Strangers do not have the desire to be changed by the therapist. Instead, they desire to incorporate the therapist into their lives.

And it is only now that I come to my point. Many Strangers are the real religious devotees of our time. Many Strangers have an insatiable yearning to worship a metaphysical figure, to seek God. They have skipped centuries of our history, have rejected pure empiricism, and have never accepted the death of God. Indeed they will secretly transform into a God any human being who offers love but remains veiled in mystery. They must indeed be thirsty for worship if they can worship a psychotherapist who may not even be an especially admirable person, who may not show any real love for the worshipper, may feel vastly superior to the Stranger, and may abuse the Stranger's thirst for worship by selling himself for a high price as an idol.

In contrast, many "normal" Natives of our time do not even admit or recognize their religious needs. These needs often remain unconscious or veiled: what Viktor Frankl calls "religious bashfulness." They deny a profound and essential part of their real nature as human beings:

> *Thou has made us for Thee*
> *And our hearts will not be at rest until they rest*
> *in Thee.—St. Augustine*

Accepting this, then, we can see that of all people in our contemporary society—empirical, scientific, materialistic and manipulative as it is—those Strangers who tirelessly seek their God offer a glimpse of a creative model for existence.

Those Strangers in society find those potentialities which the Native has neglected.

Let me tell you about a conversation between a Stranger and her Freudian analyst. The Stranger had very limited finances. She earned a small salary which she used to support herself, to contribute to the support of her mother, and to pay for her analysis. She was content with this arrangement as a temporary condition and viewed the goal of becoming more affluent as a side issue rather than as a main goal. The therapist considered her lack of economic ambition "neurotic." He said, "The fact that you are content living in a furnished room eating in cheap restaurants, and owning a minimum amount of clothes shows that you get all your satisfaction from your fantasies rather than from reality. Other people desire to buy a house, a car, pretty clothes, and they care about owning nice silver rather than the dimestore forks and knives which you bought yesterday." In order to understand the significance of this statement, you need to know that this Stranger's life was taken up with highly fulfilling activities. First, she was being psychoanalyzed, which means that her life was filled with worship. Second, she had a highly fulfilling relationship, which reached an unusual degree of affection and compatibility, with her lover. Finally, she experienced her teaching as a calling, and her positive influence on her students indicated that this perception was not fantasy, but reality. But, according to her analyst she was sick because her life did not conform to the materialistic values of mainstream society. My son, you must have guessed that this Stranger was I.

A conventional life with conventional goals rarely appeals to a Stranger. When he is told what he is missing by not pursuing money, permanent friendships, lasting sexual relations, family fun, and other American activities, he tends to wonder whether all such goals are enough to give up his mad, searching, unpredictable life with all its adversities. His life may be painful at times, but it is uniquely his. He has a deep conviction that this is the way he is meant to live.

One author, a psychotherapist, describes the Stranger as being willing to give up everything beyond the bare necessities of life. He then continues by saying that the Stranger would even go so far as to lower his social status and to associate with people of a lower socioeconomic level. Is it not shocking that a psychiatrist considers it the ultimate sacrifice to associate with people of lower status? Is it not true that people of lower status with regard to income and education are often people of higher status with regard to friendship, love and faith? Jesus must have been a Stranger, for he said: "Inasmuch as ye have done it unto one of the least of these my brethren, ye have done it unto me" (Matthew 25:40). Thus, we are at times confronted with the remarkable situation in which a Native attempts to "cure" a person of a higher spiritual and moral nature than he. Is it not that at these times the blind attempt to lead the one-eyed?

My son, had you been born we would have spent much time talking together, trying to help each other understand the nature of Strangers and Natives, wondering how the two can communicate with each other. For, after all, it is important for us to know what kind of people we Strangers are and what we can give each other and to Natives. But things being as they are, I have to do my studying alone, with only the shadow of your eternal presence shimmering by my side.

My studies at the university were often painful because my teachers were Natives; their words and their books described us as crippled and diseased. And, on the one hand, they were right, because there are so many things we cannot do which seem to come so easily to the Natives. But then, there are often things which come quite naturally to us which Natives find extremely hard to do. In so many ways, some of which I mentioned earlier, we Strangers seem to compensate for features which are missing in the world of Natives, and, in turn, Natives emphasize the aspects of life which are alien to us. It would take many volumes to elaborate on all the apects of life in which this is the case. But the most important contrast between our hosts and us is perhaps their emphasis on the drama of life which occurs in the external world versus our emphasis on the drama of life which occurs within us. Perhaps all other differences are only special aspects of this main one.

Unfortunately, in almost every case the Native's ways tend to be viewed as valid, realistic, healthy, and constructive, while the Stranger's ways tend to be viewed in a negative light in the society at large. This is only natural, since Natives are in the majority.

Thus, you, being a Stranger, would have found yourself frequently pushed to the outer fringes of society. You probably would have found yourself rejected and misunderstood in a great variety of ways. There are *two manners* in which you might have responded to your minority status.

First, you could have repressed or denied everything in you that is mad, irrational, childish, and dreamlike in order to pretend to be like the Natives. Then you might have led a life undistinguished from many other lives and you might even have attained a considerable amount of success, such as I have. But as you grew older, you would gradually—at first only faintly, then strongly, and later unbearably—become haunted by the feeling that you have played a role rather than lived a life. This is the first thing you might have done with your life as a Stranger. This is what I have done with mine.

But, there is a second way in which you might have lived. You could have become a revolutionary. You could have actively worked to overthrow

146

the views of those Natives who call us evil and ill. Like Blacks and women in my day, you could have joined hands with your brothers and sisters and marched in peaceful rebellion against those who would reject us, scorn us and use us. And like monks in a religious order, you might express, in the world that you were part of, an order too—one which preserves the dreams, the values, and the ways of life which Natives have lost, and which we would most willingly restore to them. We can accept their scorn, my son, or we can march. And I would have marched with you—had you been born—step by step, myself a Stranger and the mother of a Stranger. I would have marched right by your side down the liberating road of life.

Here ends my letter to you, my unborn schizophrenic son. It is dated the Fourth of July. The Day of Independence is a good day to write to you. To spend time all by oneself, writing to an unborn son, while other mothers take their born sons out to play, is strange indeed. It may be strange, but it is neither sick nor is it evil. It is just different, but filled with purpose and meaning: if thousands and thousands of voices would tell the world that we are their sisters and their brothers, then someday you will be born. Not to myself, for I am too old. But of a lovely and determined young woman, who will be proud to be the mother of a Stranger.

Publications by Edith Weisskopf-Joelson

With E. Frenkel-Brunswik. *Wunsch und Pflicht in Aufbau des menschlichen Lebens (Desire and Obligation in the Structure of Human Life)*. Vienna: Gerold, 1937.

"The Influence of the Time Factor on Rorschach Performances." *Rorschach Research Exchange* 6 (1942): 128–36.

"Temper Tantrums." In *Encyclopedia of Child Guidance,* edited by R. B. Wynn. New York: Philosophical Library, 1943.

"The Influence of Mental Hygiene on Intellectual Development." *Public Welfare in Indiana* 55 (1945): 19–20.

"Experimental Study of the Effect of Brightness and Ambiguity on Projection in the Thematic Apperception Test." *Journal of Psychology* 29 (1950): 407–16.

"A Transcendence Index as a Proposed Measure in the TAT." *Journal of Psychology* 29 (1950): 379–90.

With Jorge Dieppe. "Experimentally Induced Faking of TAT Responses." *Journal of Consulting Psychology* 15 (1951): 469–74.

"Intellectual Malfunctioning and Personality." *Journal of Abnormal and Social Psychology* 46 (1951): 410–23.

"Some Comments Concerning the Role of Education in the 'Creation of Creation'." *Journal of Educational Psychology* 42 (1951): 185–89.

With George P. Dunlevy, Jr. "Bodily Similarity between Subject and Central Figure in the TAT as an Influence on Projection." *Journal of Abnormal and Social Psychology* 47 (1952): 440–45.

"Early Childhood." In *Progress in Clinical Psychology,* vol. 1, edited by D. Brower and L. E. Abt. New York: Grune and Stratton, 1952.

With David P. Lynn. "The Effect of Variations in Ambiguity on Projection in the Children's Apperception Test." *Journal of Consulting Psychology* 17 (1953): 67–70.

With Lester Money, Jr. "Facial Similarity between Subject and Central Figure in the TAT as an Influence on Projection." *Journal of Abnormal and Social Psychology* 49 (1953): 341–44.

"Some Speculations Concerning the Selection of Clinical Psychologists." *Journal of Abnormal and Social Psychology* 50 (1953): 697–99.

"Some Comments on a Viennese School of Psychiatry." *Journal of Abnormal and Social Psychology* 31 (1955): 701–3.

"Creative Thinking." *Journal of the American Society of Training Directors* 11 (1957): 7–13.

With Kenneth Albrecht, Jr., E. J. Ascher, and Martin I. Hoffman. "An Experimental Investigation of 'Label Avoidance' as a Manifestation of Repression." *Journal of Projective Techniques* 21 (1957): 88–93.

With L. S. Abrahamson, H. P. David, H. Feifel, P. Forer, and R. Grundlach. "Symposium: Research with Projective Techniques." *Journal of Projective Techniques* 21 (1957): 341–61.

"Logotherapy and Existential Analysis." *Acta Psychotherapeutica* 6 (1958): 193–204.

"Some Suggestions Concerning Weltanschauung and Psychotherapy." *Journal of Abnormal and Social Psychology* 48 (1958): 601–4.

With Thomas Eliseo. "An Experimental Study of the Effectiveness of Brainstorming." *Journal of Applied Psychology* 45 (1961): 45–49.

"An Antidote against Separation." *Review of Existentialist Psychology and Psychiatry* 2 (1962): 265–83.

With H. C. Foster. "An Experimental Study of the Effect of Stimulus Variation upon Projection." *Journal of Projective Techniques* 26 (1962): 366–70.

"Paranoia and the Will-to-Meaning." *Existentialist Psychotherapy* 1 (1966): 316–20.

"Some Comments on the Psychology of Misunderstanding." *Journal of Individual Psychology* 22 (1966): 201–3.

"Meaning as an Integrating Factor." In *The Course of Human Life,* edited by Charlotte Bühler and Fred Massarik. Berlin: Springer Publishing Company, 1968.

"Mental Health and Intention." *Journal of Psychology* 69 (1968): 101–6.

"The Present Crisis in Psychotherapy." *Journal of Psychology* 69 (1968): 107–15.

With Sarah A. Alleman, Jan M. Anderson, and Steven Katkin. "Relative Emphasis on Nine Values by a Group of College Students." *Psychological Reports* 24 (1969): 299–310.

With Lois B. Wexner. "Projection as a Function of Situational and Figural Similarity." *Journal of Projective Techniques and Personality Assessment* 34 (1970): 397–400.

With Max McDaniel and Jay Zimmerman. "Similarity between Subject and Stimulus as an Influence on Projection." *Journal of Projective Techniques and Personality Assessment* 34 (1970): 328–31.

"On Surrender." *Journal of Psychology* 76 (1970): 57–66.

With Steven Katkin. "Relationship between Professed Values and Emotional Adjustment of College Students." *Psychological Reports* 28 (1971): 523–28.

"Der Sinn als integrierender Faktor." In *Lebenslauf und Lebensziele: Psychologische Studien in humanistischer Sicht,* edited by Charlotte Bühler and Fred Massarik. Stuttgart: Gustav Fischer, 1971.

"Some Comments on the Psychology of the Psychologist." *Journal of Psychology* 78 (1971): 95–114.

"Some Suggestions Concerning the Concept of Awareness." *Psychotherapy* 8 (1971): 2–7.

With Douglas O. McKeown. "The Effect of the Need Achievement on Verbal Operant Conditioning." *Journal of Psychology* 81 (1972): 23–35.

"Experimental Studies of 'Meaning'." *Annals of the New York Academy of Sciences* 193 (1972): 260–72.

With Walter F. Heiney. "Verbal Operant Conditioning as a Measure of Value Strength I." *Journal of Psychology* 80 (1972): 45–56.

With Wayne Matthey. "Verbal Operant Conditioning as a Measure of Value Strength II: The Use of Values as Reinforced Response Classes." *Journal of Psychology* 81 (1972): 13–22.

"Logotherapy: Science or Faith?" *Psychotherapy* 12 (1975): 238–40.

"Viktor E. Frankl," the first of "Six Representative Approaches to Existential Therapy." In *Existential-Phenomenological Alternatives for Psychology,* edited by Ronald S. Valle and Mark King. New York: Oxford University Press, 1978.

"The Place of Logotherapy in the World Today." *The International Forum for Logotherapy* 3 (1980): 3–7.

"Values: The Enfant Terrible of Psychotherapy." *Psychotherapy* 17 (1980): 459–66.

"My Work." In *The Women in Psychology,* edited by G. Stevens and S. Gardner. Cambridge: Schenkman, 1982.

"The Role of Philosophy in Five Kinds of Therapeutic Systems" and "The Therapeutic Ingredients of Religious and Political Philosophies." In *Philosophy and Therapy,* edited by P. W. Sharkey. Washington, D.C.: University Press of America, 1982.

"Remarks of a Free-Floating Spirit." *The International Forum for Logotherapy* 6 (1983): 98–101.